EIGER DREAMS

EIGER DREAMS

Ventures Among Men and Mountains

JON KRAKAUER

LYONS & BURFORD
PUBLISHERS

Portions of this book have appeared previously: "Eiger Dreams," in *Outside*, March 1985; "Gill," in *New Age Journal*, March 1985; "Valdez Ice," in *Smithsonian*, January 1988; "On Being Tentbound," in *Outside*, October 1982; "The Flyboys of Talkeetna," in *Smithsonian*, January 1989; "Club Denali," in *Outside*, December 1987; "Chamonix," in *Outside*, July 1989; "Canyoneering," in *Outside*, October 1988; "A Mountain Higher than Everest?" in *Smithsonian*, October 1987; "The Burgess Boys," in *Outside*, August 1988; "A Bad Summer of K2," in *Outside*, March 1987 (Cowritten with Greg Child).

Printed in the United States of America

10 9 8 7 6 5 4 3 2

LIBRARY OF CONGRESS
CATALOGING-IN-PUBLICATION DATA

Krakauer, Jon.
    Eiger dreams : ventures among men and mountains / Jon Krakauer.
        p.   cm.
ISBN 1-55821-057-1 (cloth); ISBN 1-55821-411-9 (paperback)
    1. Mountaineering.   I. Title.
    GV200.K73   1990   89-77021
    796.5'22—dc20   CIP

▲ *For* LINDA, *with thoughts of Green Mountain Falls,*
the Wind Rivers, and Roanoke Street.

The oldest, most widespread stories in the world are adventure stories, about human heroes who venture into the myth-countries at the risk of their lives, and bring back tales of the world beyond men . . . It could be argued . . . that the narrative art itself arose from the need to tell an adventure; that man risking his life in perilous encounters constitutes the original definition of what is worth talking about.

Paul Zweig
THE ADVENTURER

△

Having an adventure shows that someone is incompetent, that something has gone wrong. An adventure is interesting enough in retrospect, especially to the person who didn't have it; at the time it happens it usually constitutes an exceedingly disagreeable experience.

Vilhjalmur Stefansson
MY LIFE WITH THE ESKIMO

CONTENTS

AUTHOR'S NOTE

MOUNTAIN CLIMBING IS COMPREHENDED DIMLY, IF AT ALL, BY MOST of the nonclimbing world. It's a favorite subject for bad movies and spurious metaphors. A dream about scaling some high, jagged alp is something a shrink can really sink his teeth into. The activity is wrapped in tales of audacity and disaster that make other sports out to be trivial games by comparison; as an idea, climbing strikes that chord in the public imagination most often associated with sharks and killer bees.

It is the aim of this book to prune away some of this overgrown mystique—to let in a little light. Most climbers aren't in fact deranged, they're just infected with a particularly virulent strain of the Human Condition.

In the interest of truth in packaging, I should state straightaway that nowhere does this book come right out and address the central question—Why would a normal person want to do this stuff?—head on; I circle the issue continually, poke at it from behind with a long stick now and then, but at no point do I jump right in the cage and wrestle with the beast directly, *mano a mano*. Even so, by the end of the book I think the reader will have a better sense not only of why climbers climb, but why they tend to be so goddamn obsessive about it.

I trace the roots of my own obsession back to 1962. I was a fairly ordinary kid growing up in Corvallis, Oregon. My father was a sensible, rigid parent who constantly badgered his five children to study calculus and Latin, keep their noses to the grindstone, fix their sights early and unflinchingly on careers in medicine or law.

Inexplicably, on the occasion of my eighth birthday this strict task-master presented me with a pint-size ice axe and took me on my first climb. In retrospect I can't imagine what the old man was thinking; if he'd given me a Harley and a membership in the Hell's Angels he couldn't have sabotaged his paternal aspirations any more effectively.

By the age of eighteen climbing was the only thing I cared about: work, school, friendships, career plans, sex, sleep—all were made to fit around my climbing or, more often, neglected outright. In 1974 my preoccupation intensified further still. The pivotal event was my first Alaskan expedition, a month-long trip with six companions to the Arrigetch Peaks, a knot of slender granite towers possessed of a severe, haunting beauty. One June morning at 2:30 A.M., after climbing for twelve straight hours, I pulled up onto the summit of a mountain called Xanadu. The top was a disconcertingly narrow fin of rock, likely the highest point in the whole range. And ours were the first boots ever to step upon it. Far below, the spires and slabs of the surrounding peaks glowed orange, as if lit from within, in the eerie, nightlong dusk of the arctic summer. A bitter wind screamed across the tundra from the Beaufort Sea, turning my hands to wood. I was as happy as I'd ever been in my life.

I graduated from college, by the skin of my teeth, in December, 1975. I spent the next eight years employed as an itinerant carpenter and commercial fisherman in Colorado, Seattle, and Alaska, living in studio apartments with cinder-block walls, driving a hundred-dollar car, working just enough to make rent and fund the next climbing trip. Eventually it began to wear thin. I found myself lying awake nights reliving all the close scrapes I'd had on the heights. Sawing joists in the rain at some muddy construction site, my thoughts would increasingly turn to college classmates who were raising families, investing in real estate, buying lawn furniture, assiduously amassing wealth.

I resolved to quit climbing, and said as much to the woman with whom I was involved at the time. She was so taken aback by this

△ ix

announcement that she agreed to marry me. I'd grossly underestimated the hold climbing had on me, however; giving it up proved much more difficult than I'd imagined. My abstinence lasted barely a year, and when it ended it looked for a while like the connubial arrangement was going to end with it. Against all odds, I somehow managed to stay married *and* keep climbing. No longer, however, did I feel compelled to push things right to the brink, to see God on every pitch, to make each climb more radical than the last. Today I feel like an alcoholic who's managed to make the switch from week-long whiskey benders to a few beers on Saturday night. I've slipped happily into alpine mediocrity.

My ambitions as a climber have been inversely proportional to my efforts as a writer. In 1981 I sold my first article to a national magazine; in November, 1983, I bought a word processor, took off my tool belt for what I hoped would be the last time, and began writing for a living. I've been at it full-time ever since. These days more and more of my assignments seem to be about architecture, or natural history, or popular culture—I've written about fire walking for *Rolling Stone*, wigs for *Smithsonian*, neo-Régency design for *Architectural Digest*—but mountaineering stories continue to be nearest and dearest to my heart.

Eleven of the twelve essays collected between these covers were initially written for magazines (the closing story, "The Devils Thumb," was written specifically for this book). As such, they have benefited—and occasionally suffered—from the attentions of a small army of editors and fact checkers at the publications that first put the articles into print. I am especially indebted to Mark Bryant and John Rasmus at *Outside*, and Jack Wiley, Jim Doherty, and Don Moser at *Smithsonian*, for the invaluable contributions they've made to the best of these pieces. All five men are accomplished writers as well as superb editors, and it showed in the sensitivity and restraint they demonstrated time and time again in their efforts to steer me right when I was going wrong.

I also owe thanks to Larry Burke, Mike McRae, Dave Schonauer,

Todd Balf, Alison Carpenter Davis, Marilyn Johnson, Michelle Stacey, Liz Kaufmann, Barbara Rowley, Susan Campbell, Larry Evans, Joe Crump, Laura Hohnhold, Lisa Chase, Sue Smith, Matthew Childs, and Rob Story at *Outside*; Caroline Despard, Ed Rich, Connie Bond, Judy Harkison, Bruce Hathaway, Tim Foote, and Frances Glennon at *Smithsonian*; Phil Zaleski and David Abramson at *New Age Journal*; H. Adams Carter at *The American Alpine Journal*; Michael Kennedy and Alsion Osius at *Climbing*; Ken Wilson at *Mountain*; Peter Burford for his hand in shaping this collection; Deborah Shaw and Nick Miller for their hospitality; my agent John Ware; and fellow freelancer Greg Child, with whom I collaborated on an early draft of "A Bad Summer on K2."

For sharing a rope during some memorable days in the mountains I'm grateful to Fritz Wiessner, Bernd Arnold, David Trione, Ed Trione, Tom Davies, Marc Francis Twight, Mark Fagan, Dave Jones, Matt Hale, Chris Gulick, Laura Brown, Jack Tackle, Yvon Chouinard, Lou Dawson, Roman Dial, Kate Bull, Brian Teale, John Weiland, Bob Shelton, Nate Zinsser, Larry Bruce, Molly Higgins, Pam Brown, Bill Bullard, Helen Apthorp, Jeff White, Holly Crary, Ben Reed, Mark Rademacher, Jim Balog, Mighty Joe Hladick, Scott Johnston, Mark Hesse, Chip Lee, Henry Barber, Pete Athans, Harry Kent, Dan Cauthorn, and Robert Gully.

Most of all, I'd like to thank Lew and Carol Krakauer for having the poor judgment to take their eight-year-old son up the South Sister; Steve Rottler for hiring and rehiring me over so many years in Boulder, Seattle, and Port Alexander; Ed Ward, the most naturally gifted climber I have ever seen, who showed me how to climb hard and stay alive doing it; David Roberts, who introduced me to Alaska and taught me how to write; and Linda Mariam Moore, my best editor and closest pal.

1. EIGER DREAMS

IN THE EARLY MOMENTS OF *The Eiger Sanction*, CLINT EASTWOOD saunters into the dimly lit headquarters of C-2 to find out who he is supposed to assassinate next. Dragon, the evil albino who runs the CIA-like organization, tells Eastwood that although the agency does not yet have the target's name, they have discovered that "our man will be involved in a climb in the Alps this summer. And we know which mountain he will climb: the Eiger."

Eastwood has no trouble guessing which route—"The North Face, of course"—and allows that he is familiar with that particular alpine wall: "I tried to climb it twice, it tried to kill me twice . . . Look, if the target's trying to climb the Eiger, chances are my work will be done for me."

The problem with climbing the North Face of the Eiger is that in addition to getting up 6,000 vertical feet of crumbling limestone and black ice, one must climb over some formidable mythology. The trickiest moves on any climb are the mental ones, the psychological gymnastics that keep terror in check, and the Eiger's grim aura is intimidating enough to rattle anyone's poise. The epics that have taken place on the Nordwand have been welded into the world's collective unconscious in grisly detail by more than two thousand newspaper and magazine articles. The dust jackets of books with titles such as *Eiger: Wall of Death*, remind us that the Nordwand "has defeated hundreds and killed forty-four . . . Those who fell were found—sometimes years later—dessicated and dismembered. The body of one Italian mountaineer hung from its rope, unreachable but visible to the curious below, for three years,

▲ 1

alternately sealed into the ice sheath of the wall and swaying in the winds of summer."

The history of the mountain resonates with the struggles of such larger-than-life figures as Buhl, Bonatti, Messner, Rebuffat, Terray, Haston, and Harlin, not to mention Eastwood. The names of the landmarks on the face—the Hinterstoisser Traverse, the Ice Hose, the Death Bivouac, the White Spider—are household words among both active and armchair alpinists from Tokyo to Buenos Aires; the very mention of these places is enough to make any climber's hands turn clammy. The rockfall and avalanches that rain continuously down the Nordwand are legendary. So is the heavy weather: Even when the skies over the rest of Europe are cloudless, violent storms brew over the Eiger, like those dark clouds that hover eternally above Transylvanian castles in vampire movies.

Needless to say, all this makes the Eiger North Face one of the most widely coveted climbs in the world.

The Nordwand was first climbed in 1938, and since then it has had more than 150 ascents, among them a solo climb in 1983 that took all of five and a half hours, but don't try to tell Staff Sergeant Carlos J. Ragone, U.S.A.F., that the Eiger has become a scenic cruise. Last fall, Marc Twight and I were sitting outside our tents above Kleine Scheidegg, the cluster of hotels and restaurants at the foot of the Eiger, when Ragone strolled into camp under a bulging pack and announced that he had come to climb the Nordwand. In the discussion that ensued, we learned that he was AWOL from an air base in England. His commanding officer had refused to grant Ragone a leave when the C.O. learned what Ragone intended to do with it, but Ragone had left anyway. "Trying this climb will probably cost me my stripes," he said, "but on the other hand, if I get up the mother they might promote me."

Unfortunately, Ragone didn't get up the mother. September had gone down in the Swiss record books as the wettest since 1864, and the face was in atrocious condition, worse even than usual, plastered with rime and loaded with unstable snow. The weather

△ 2

forecast was for continuing snow and high wind. Two partners who were supposed to rendezvous with Ragone backed out because of the nasty conditions. Ragone, however, was not about to be deterred by the mere lack of company. On October 3 he started up the climb by himself. On the lower reaches of the face, near the top of a buttress known as the First Pillar, he made a misstep. His ice axes and crampons sheared out of the rotten ice, and Ragone found himself airborne. Five hundred vertical feet later he hit the ground.

Incredibly, his landing was cushioned by the accumulation of powder snow at the base of the wall, and Ragone was able to walk away from the fall with no more damage than bruises and a crimp in his back. He hobbled out of the blizzard into the *Bahnhof buffet*, asked for a room, went upstairs, and fell asleep. At some point during his tumble to the bottom of the wall he had lost an ice axe and his wallet, which contained all his identification and money. In the morning, when it was time to settle his room bill, all Ragone could offer for payment was his remaining ice axe. The *Bahnhof* manager was not amused. Before slinking out of Scheidegg, Ragone stopped by our camp to ask if we were interested in buying what was left of his climbing gear. We told him that we'd like to help him out, but we happened to be a little strapped for cash ourselves. In that case, Ragone, seeing as he didn't think he was going to feel like climbing again for a while, said he'd just give the stuff to us. "That mountain is a bastard," he spat, glancing up at the Nordwand one last time. With that, he limped off through the snow toward England to face the wrath of his C.O.

Like Ragone, Marc and I had come to Switzerland to climb the Nordwand. Marc, eight years my junior, sports two earrings in his left ear and a purple haircut that would do a punk rocker proud. He is also a red-hot climber. One of the differences between us was that Marc wanted very badly to climb the Eiger, while I wanted very badly only to have climbed the Eiger. Marc, understand, is

△ 3

at that age when the pituitary secretes an overabundance of those hormones that mask the subtler emotions, such as fear. He tends to confuse things like life-or-death climbing with fun. As a friendly gesture, I planned to let Marc lead all the most fun pitches on the Nordwand.

Unlike Ragone, Marc and I were not willing to go up on the wall until conditions improved. Due to the Nordwand's concave architecture, whenever it snows, few places on the wall are not exposed to avalanches. In summer, if things go well, it will typically take a strong party two days, maybe three, to climb the Nordwand. In the fall, with the shorter days and icier conditions, three to four days is the norm. To maximize our chances of getting up and down the Eiger without unpleasant incident, we figured we needed at least four consecutive days of good weather: one day to allow the buildup of new snow to avalanche off, and three to climb the face and descend the mountain's west flank.

Each morning during our stay at Scheidegg we would crawl out of our tents, plow down through the snowdrifts to the *Bahnhof*, and phone Geneva and Zurich to get a four-day weather forecast. Day after day, the word was the same: Continuing unsettled weather, with rain in the valleys and snow in the mountains. We could do nothing but curse and wait, and the waiting was awful. The Eiger's mythic weight bore down especially hard during the idle days, and it was easy to think too much.

One afternoon, for diversion, we took a ride on the train up to the *Jungfraujoch*, a cog railroad that runs from Kleine Scheidegg to a saddle high on the Eiger-Jungfrau massif. This turned out to be a mistake. The railway traverses the bowels of the Eiger by way of a tunnel that was blasted through the mountain in 1912. Midway up the tracks there is an intermediate station with a series of huge windows that look out from the vertical expanse of the Nordwand.

The view from these windows is so vertiginous that barf bags—the same kind they put in airplane seat-pockets—had been placed on the windowsills. Clouds swirled just beyond the glass. The black rock of the Nordwand, sheathed in frost feathers and sprouting icicles in the places where it overhung, fell away dizzyingly into the mists below. Small avalanches hissed past. If our route turned out to be anything like what we were seeing, we were going to find ourselves in serious trouble. Climbing in such conditions would be desperate if not impossible.

On the Eiger, constructions of the imagination have a way of blurring with reality, and the Eigerwand station was a little too much like a scene from a recurring dream I've been having for years in which I'm fighting for my life in a storm on some endless climb when I come upon a door set into the mountainside. The doorway leads into a warm room with a fireplace and tables of steaming food and a comfortable bed. Usually, in this dream, the door is locked.

A quarter-mile down the tunnel from the big windows of the midway station there is in fact a small wooden door—always unlocked—that opens out onto the Nordwand. The standard route up the wall passes very near this door, and more than one climber has used it to escape from a storm.

Such an escape, however, poses hazards of its own. In 1981, Mugs Stump, one of America's most accomplished alpinists, popped in through the door after a storm forced him to abort a solo attempt on the wall and started walking toward the tunnel entrance, about a mile away. Before he could reach daylight, he met a train coming up the tracks. The guts of the Eiger are hard black limestone that makes for tough tunneling, and when the tunnel was constructed the builders didn't make it any wider than they had to. It quickly became evident to Stump that the space between the cars and the tunnel walls was maybe a foot, give or take a few inches. The Swiss take great pride in making their trains run on time, and it also became evident that this particular engineer was not about to foul up his schedule simply because some damn climber was on the tracks. All Stump could do was suck in his breath, press up

△ 5

against the rock, and try to make his head thin. He survived the train's passing, but the experience was as harrowing as any of the close scrapes he'd had on the outside of the mountain.

During our third week of waiting for the weather to break, Marc and I rode the train down into Wengen and Lauterbrunnen to find relief from the snow. After a pleasant day of taking in the sights and sipping *Rugenbrau*, we managed to miss the last train up to Scheidegg and were faced with a long walk back to the tents. Marc set out at a blistering pace to try to make camp before dark, but I decided I was in no hurry to get back under the shadow of the Eiger and into the snow zone, and that another beer or two would make the hike easier to endure.

It was dark by the time I left Wengen, but the Oberland trails, though steep (the Swiss, it seems, do not believe in switchbacks) are wide, well maintained, and easy to follow. More important, on this path there were none of the electrified gates that Marc and I had encountered on a rainy night the week before (after missing another train) while walking from Grindelwald to Scheidegg. Such gates are installed to curtail bovine trespassers and are impossible to see in the dark after a few beers. They strike a five-foot nine-inch body at an uncommonly sensitive point precisely six inches below the belt, and with one's feet clad in soggy Nikes they deliver a jolt of sufficient voltage to bring forth confessions to crimes not yet committed.

The walk from Wengen went without incident until I neared the treeline, when I began to hear an intermittent roar that sounded like someone goosing the throttle of a Boeing 747. The first gust of wind hit me when I rounded the shoulder of the Lauberhorn and turned toward Wengernalp. A blast came from out of nowhere and knocked me on my butt. It was the *foehn*, blowing down from the Eiger.

The *foehn* winds of the Bernese Oberland—cousin of the Santa Ana winds that periodically set Southern California on fire and the

△ 6

chinooks that roar down out of the Colorado Rockies—can generate stunning power. They are said to hold a disproportionate number of positive ions, and to make people crazy. "In Switzerland," Joan Didion writes in *Slouching Towards Bethlehem*, "the suicide rate goes up during the *foehn*, and in the courts of some Swiss cantons the wind is considered a mitigating circumstance for crime." The *foehn* figures prominently in Eiger lore. It is a dry, relatively warm wind, and as it melts the snow and ice on the Eiger it brings down terrible avalanches. Typically, immediately following a *foehnsturm* there will be a sharp freeze, glazing the wall with treacherous verglas. Many of the disasters on the Nordwand can be attributed directly to the *foehn*; in *The Eiger Sanction* it is a *foehn* that almost does Eastwood in.

It was all I could do to handle the *foehn* on the trail through the cow pastures. I shuddered to think what it would be like to be hit by one up on the Nordwand. The wind filled my eyes with grit and blew me off my feet over and over again. Several times I simply had to get down on my knees and wait for lulls between gusts. When I finally lurched through the door of the *Bahnhof* at Scheidegg, I found the place packed with railroad workers, cooks, maids, waitresses, and tourists who had become marooned by the storm. The gale raging outside had infected everybody in Scheidegg with some kind of weird, manic energy, and a riotous party was in full swing. In one corner people were dancing to a screaming jukebox, in another they were standing on the tables belting out German drinking songs; everywhere people were calling the waiter for more beer and schnapps.

I was about to join the fun when I spied Marc approaching with a wild look in his eyes. "Jon," he blurted out, "the tents are gone!"

"Hey, I don't really want to deal with it right now," I replied, trying to signal the waiter, "Let's just rent beds upstairs tonight and repitch the tents in the morning."

"No, no, you don't understand. They didn't just get knocked down, they fucking blew away. I found the yellow one about fifty yards away from where it had been, but the brown one is gone, man. I looked but I couldn't find it anywhere. It's probably down in Grindelwald by now."

The tents had been tied down to logs, cement blocks, and an ice screw driven securely into frozen turf. There had been at least two hundred pounds of food and gear inside them. It seemed impossible that they could have been carried away by the wind, but they had. The one that was missing had contained our sleeping bags, clothing, my climbing boots, the stove and pots, some food, God only knew what else. If we didn't find it, the weeks of waiting to climb the Nordwand were going to be in vain, so I zipped up my jacket and headed back out into the _foehnsturm_.

By sheer chance I found the tent a quarter-mile from where it had been pitched—drifted over, lying in the middle of the train tracks to Grindelwald. It was a tangled mess of shredded nylon and broken, twisted poles. After wrestling it back to the _Bahnhof_, we discovered that the stove had sprayed butane over everything, and a dozen eggs had coated our clothing and sleeping bags with a nasty, sulphurous slime, but it appeared that no important gear had been lost during the tent's tour of Scheidegg. We threw everything in a corner and returned to the party to celebrate.

The winds at Scheidegg that night were clocked at 170 kilometers per hour. In addition to laying waste to our camp, they knocked down the big telescope on the gift-shop balcony and blew a ski-lift gondola as big as a truck onto the tracks in front of the _Bahnhof_. At midnight, though, the gale petered out. The temperature plummeted, and by morning a foot of fresh powder had replaced the snowpack melted by the _foehn_. Nevertheless, when we called the weather station in Geneva, we were shocked to hear that an extended period of good weather would be arriving in a couple of days. "Sweet Jesus," I thought. "We're actually going to have to go up on the wall."

The sunshine came on October 8, along with a promise from the meteorologists that there would be no precipitation for at least five

△ 8

days. We gave the Nordwand the morning to slough off the post-*foehn* accumulation of snow, then hiked through crotch-deep drifts over to the base of the route, where we set up a hastily patched-together tent. We were in our sleeping bags early, but I was too scared to even pretend to sleep.

At 3 A.M., the appointed hour to start up the wall, it was raining and some major ice and rockfall was strafing the face. The climb was off. Secretly relieved, I went back to bed and immediately sank into a deep slumber. I awoke at 9 A.M. to the sound of birds chirping. The weather had turned perfect once again. Hurriedly, we threw our packs together. As we started up the Nordwand my stomach felt like a dog had been chewing on it all night.

We had been told by friends who had climbed the Nordwand that the first third of the standard route up the face is "way casual." It isn't, at least not under the conditions we found it. Although there were few moves that were technically difficult, the climbing was continuously insecure. A thin crust of ice lay over deep, unstable powder snow. It was easy to see how Ragone had fallen; it felt as though at any moment the snow underfoot was going to collapse. In places where the wall steepened, the snow cover thinned and our ice axes would ricochet off rock a few inches beneath the crust. It was impossible to find anchors of any kind in or under the rotting snow and ice, so for the first two thousand feet of the climb we simply left the ropes in the packs and "soloed" together.

Our packs were cumbersome and threatened to pull us over backward whenever we would lean back to search out the route above. We had made an effort to pare our loads down to the essentials, but Eiger terror had moved us to throw in extra food, fuel, and clothing in case we got pinned down by a storm, and enough climbing hardware to sink a ship. It had been difficult to decide what to take and what to leave behind. Marc eventually elected to bring along a Walkman and his two favorite tapes instead of a sleeping bag, reasoning that when the going got desperate, the peace of mind to be had by listening to the Dead Kennedys and

△ 9

the Angry Samoans would prove more valuable than staying warm at night.

At 4 P.M., when we reached the overhanging slab called the Rote Fluh, we were finally able to place some solid anchors, the first ones of the climb. The overhang offered protection from the unidentified falling objects that occasionally hummed past, so we decided to stop and bivouac even though there was more than an hour of daylight left. By digging out a long, narrow platform where the snow slope met the rock, we could lie in relative comfort, head-to-head, with the stove between us.

The next morning we got up at three and were away from our little ledge an hour before dawn, climbing by headlamp. A rope-length beyond the bivouac, Marc started leading up a pitch that had a difficulty rating of 5.4. Marc is a 5.12 climber, so I was alarmed when he began to mutter and his progress came to a halt. He tried moving left, and then right, but an eggshell-thin layer of crumbly ice over the vertical rock obscured whatever holds there might have been. Agonizingly slowly, he balanced his way upward a few inches at a time by hooking his crampon points and the picks of his axes on unseen limestone nubbins underneath the patina of rime. Five times he slipped, but caught himself each time after falling only a few feet.

Two hours passed while Marc thrashed around above me. The sun came up. I grew impatient. "Marc," I yelled, "if you don't want to lead this one, come on down and I'll take a shot at it." The bluff worked: Marc attacked the pitch with renewed determination and was soon over it. When I joined him at his belay stance, though, I was worried. It had taken us nearly three hours to climb eighty feet. There is more than eight thousand feet of climbing on the Nordwand (when all the traversing is taken into consideration), and much of it was going to be a lot harder than those eighty feet.

The next pitch was the infamous Hinterstoisser Traverse, a 140-foot end run around some unclimbable overhangs, and the key to gaining the upper part of the Nordwand. It was first climbed in

1936 by Andreas Hinterstoisser, whose lead across its polished slabs was a brilliant piece of climbing. But above the pitch he and his three companions were caught by a storm and forced to retreat. The storm, however, had glazed the traverse with verglas, and the climbers were unable to reverse its delicate moves. All four men perished. Since that disaster, climbers have always taken pains to leave a rope fixed across the traverse to ensure return passage.

We found the slabs of the Hinterstoisser covered with two inches of ice. Thin though it was, it was solid enough to hold our ice axes if we swung them gently. Additionally, an old, frayed fixed rope emerged intermittently from the glazing. By crabbing gingerly across the ice on our front points and shamelessly grabbing the old rope whenever possible, we got across the traverse without a hitch.

Above the Hinterstoisser, the route went straight up, past landmarks that had been the stuff of my nightmares since I was ten: the Swallow's Nest, the First Icefield, the Ice Hose. The climbing never again got as difficult as the pitch Marc had led just before the Hinterstoisser, but we were seldom able to get in any anchors. A slip by either of us would send us both to the bottom of the wall.

As the day wore on, I could feel my nerves beginning to unravel. At one point, while leading over crusty, crumbly vertical ice on the Ice Hose, I suddenly became overwhelmed by the fact that the only things preventing me from flying off into space were two thin steel picks sunk half an inch into a medium that resembled the inside of my freezer when it needs to be defrosted. I looked down at the ground more than three thousand feet below and felt dizzy, as if I were about to faint. I had to close my eyes and take a dozen deep breaths before I could resume climbing.

One 165-foot pitch past the Ice Hose brought us to the bottom of the Second Ice Field, a point slightly more than halfway up the wall. Above, the first protected place to spend the night would be the Death Bivouac, the ledge where Max Sedlmayer and Karl Mehringer had expired in a storm during the first attempt on the Nordwand in 1935. Despite its grim name, the Death Bivouac is probably

△ 11

the safest and most comfortable bivouac site on the face. To get to it, however, we still had to make an eighteen-hundred-foot rising traverse across the Second Ice Field, and then ascend several hundred devious feet more to the top of a buttress called the Flatiron.

It was 1 P.M. We had climbed only about fourteen hundred feet in the eight hours since we'd left our bivouac at the Rote Fluh. Even though the Second Ice Field looked easy, the Flatiron beyond it did not, and I had serious doubts that we could make the Death Bivouac—more than two thousand feet away—in the five hours of daylight that remained. If darkness fell before we reached the Death Bivouac, we would be forced to spend the night without a ledge, in a place that would be completely exposed to the avalanches and rocks that spilled down from the most notorious feature on the Nordwand: the ice field called the White Spider.

"Marc," I said, "we should go down."

"What?!" he replied, shocked. "Why?"

I outlined my reasons: our slow pace, the distance to the Death Bivouac, the poor condition the wall was in, the increasing avalanche hazard as the day warmed up. While we talked, small spindrift avalanches showered down over us from the Spider. After fifteen minutes, Marc reluctantly agreed that I was right, and we began our descent.

Wherever we could find anchors, we rappelled; where we couldn't, we down-climbed. At sunset, below a pitch called the Difficult Crack, Marc found a cave for us to bivouac in. By then we were already second-guessing the decision to retreat, and we spent the evening saying little to each other.

At dawn, just after resuming the descent, we heard voices coming from the face below. Two climbers soon appeared, a man and a woman, moving rapidly up the steps we had kicked two days before. It was obvious from their fluid, easy movements that they were both very, very good climbers. The man turned out to be Christophe Profit, a famous French alpinist. He thanked us for kicking

△ 12

all the steps, then the two of them sped off toward the Difficult Crack at an astonishing clip.

A day after we had wimped-out because the face was "out of condition," it appeared as though two French climbers were going to cruise up the climb as if it were a Sunday stroll. I glanced over at Marc and it looked like he was about to burst into tears. At that point we split up and continued the nerve-wracking descent by separate routes.

Two hours later I stepped down onto the snow at the foot of the wall. Waves of relief swept over me. The vise that had been squeezing my temples and gut was suddenly gone. By God, I had survived! I sat down in the snow and began to laugh.

Marc was a few hundred yards away, sitting on a rock. When I reached him I saw that he was crying, and not out of joy. In Marc's estimation, simply surviving the Nordwand did not cut it. "Hey," I heard myself telling him, "if the Frogs get up the sucker, we can always go into Wengen and buy more food, and then go for it again." Marc perked up immediately at this suggestion, and before I could retract my words he was sprinting off to the tent to monitor the French climbers' progress through binoculars.

At this point, however, my luck with the Nordwand finally took a turn for the better: Christophe Profit and his partner only got as far as the Rote Fluh, the site of our first bivouac, before a large avalanche shot past and scared them into coming down, too. A day later, before my Eiger luck could turn again, I was on a jet home.

△ 13

2. GILL

Just west of Pueblo, Colorado, the flat expanse of the Great Plains gives way to the first nascent ripples of the Rocky Mountains. Here, among the scrub oak and cactus, a massive boulder the color and texture of weathered brick rises fifteen feet above a parched meadow. The rock is much longer than it is high, with a gently overhanging flank that flares out of the sand like the rusting hull of a long-beached ship. To the untrained eye, the face of the boulder looks nearly smooth: a rounded bulge here and there, a few tiny holes, now and then a pencil-thin ledge. There appears to be no way for a person to climb this chunk of sandstone. Which is precisely what draws John Gill to it.

Gill dusts his fingers with gymnasts' chalk and walks purposefully up to the boulder's base. By clinging to small nicks on the rock's surface and balancing on pea-size nubbins, he somehow manages to pull his body off the ground, as if by levitation. To Gill, the boulder's steep face is a puzzle to be solved with finger strength, creative movement, and force of will. He puts the puzzle together piece by piece, delicately shifting his weight from tiny hold to tiny hold until he finds himself hanging from his fingertips three feet beneath the boulder's crest. Here he seems stymied; his feet dangle uselessly in space and his position is so tenuous that he can't let go with either hand to reach higher without falling.

Wearing an expression of beatific calm that gives no clue to the terrible strain his muscles are under, Gill fixes his eyes on the top, dips his shoulders slightly, and then springs suddenly for the crest from his pathetic handholds. Completely airborne, his body travels

▲ 14

upward mere inches before the apogee of its flight is reached, but in that moment, just as he begins to be pulled earthward, his left hand shoots for the crest of the boulder like a snake striking a rat and clamps onto it securely. A few seconds later Gill is standing on top.

John Gill is a living legend to mountain climbers on three continents, a man held in awe by the best in the sport. Customarily, a person gains entry into the mythology of mountaineering through death-defying deeds in the Himalaya, Alaska, the Alps, or the huge granite walls of Yosemite. Gill's reputation, though, rests entirely on ascents less than thirty feet high: He has joined the elite company of Hermann Buhl, Sir Edmund Hillary, Royal Robbins, and Reinhold Messner by ascending nothing bigger than boulders.

Make no mistake: Gill's ascents may be diminutive, but by no stretch of the imagination are they easy. The boulders he climbs tend to be overhanging and lacking in fissures or rugosities substantial enough for lesser climbers even to see, let alone stand on or cling to. In effect, Gill's climbs distill the cumulative challenges of an entire mountain into a compact chunk of granite or sandstone the size of a garbage truck or modest suburban house. It is no exaggeration to say that the summit of Mt. Everest could sooner be reached by most climbers than could the summit of any one of a score of Gill's boulders.

Actually, to Gill's mind, summits aren't even very important. The real pleasure of "bouldering" lies more in the doing than in attaining the goal. "The boulderer is concerned with form almost as much as with success," says Gill. "Bouldering isn't really a sport. It's a climbing activity with metaphysical, mystical, and philosophical overtones."

Gill is in his early fifties, a tall, trim man, with sad eyes and smooth, careful movements. He speaks the same way he moves—slowly, deliberately, with meticulously chosen words uttered in grammatically perfect sentences. With his wife Dorothy and a number of well-fed pets that he pretends to disdain, Gill lives in a plain two-story home in Pueblo, a steel town on the sun-baked southern Colorado plains that has seen better days. Except, perhaps, for somewhat oversize arms and shoulders, when Gill is standing on horizontal ground there is nothing about his demeanor or physical presence to suggest that he is a mythic figure, a man whose activities on ridiculously steep rock have led people to suggest that he has uncovered some major loophole in the laws of gravity. With his thinning hair and neatly trimmed goatee, Gill looks a lot like a mild-mannered professor of mathematics—which, it turns out, he is.

That Gill is both master boulderer and mathematician is no coincidence; he sees significant parallels between these two seemingly unrelated activities. "When I first started climbing I met several other climbers who were research mathematicians," Gill muses. "I wondered, 'Why is it that out of the few people I meet climbing, so many of them turn out to be research mathematicians?' Even though one activity is almost completely cerebral and the other is mainly physical, there is something common to bouldering and mathematical research. I think it has something to do with pattern recognition, a natural instinct to analyze a pattern."

Impossible-looking mathematical proofs, Gill says, are solved by "quantum jumps of intuition, and the same thing is true in bouldering." It is no accident that in the jargon of climbers, boulder climbs are termed "problems" (as in, "Did you hear that Kauk finally bagged that way heinous problem across the river, the one that had thrashed all the Eurodogs?").

Whether a block of overhanging sandstone or the proof of an unlikely theorem, the problems Gill relishes the most are those that have not yet been solved. "I enjoy finding a piece of rock that has never been climbed, visualizing some pattern of holds on the surface of that rock, and then climbing it. And, of course, the more obscure the pattern, the more difficult the appearance of the rock, the greater the satisfaction. There is something there that can be created, possibly, if one uses insight and intuition to make this quantum jump.

△ 16

One discovers that a bouldering route can be accomplished not by looking at each minute hold, foot by foot, but by looking at the overall problem."

For both ambitious boulderers and ambitious mathematicians, Gill emphasizes, it's not enough merely to solve a particular problem: "One of the objectives for both is to achieve an interesting result—ideally an unexpected result—in an elegant fashion, with a smooth flow, using some unexpected simplicity. There is the question of style." But beyond this, he adds, "to be a boulderer or a research mathematician you have to have this natural inclination to dig for something, a strong, completely inner motivation to be on the frontier, to discover things. The reward, in both activities, is almost continual enlightenment, and that's a great feeling."

An only child of a college professor who moved from town to town every few years, Gill describes his childhood as being "a little lonely at times. I was never athletic, I never went out for any organized sports." He spent a lot of time wandering around by himself in the woods, and enjoyed climbing trees. On family vacations when he was seven or eight, his parents tell him that he used to ask them to stop whenever the car would pass a road cut so he could scramble up it.

"In junior and senior high school," Gill continues, "I sang in the choir. I was really a pretty boring person at times." In high school in Atlanta, however, Gill met a girl who had done some climbing in the West. One weekend she invited him to accompany a group of students on a rock-climbing excursion in north Georgia. Gill watched for a while, and then gave it a try. "I was fairly klutzy," he recounts, "but I found the whole business terribly intriguing. It was the most intense thing that I'd ever done. It offered a change of perspective. Something about the rock really beckoned to me."

In 1954, after graduating from high school, he drove out to Colorado with a friend to climb for the summer. Gill may have been klutzy, but he was also bold: One day he soloed most of the way up the sheer east face of Longs Peak before a local mountain guide, thinking Gill to be some lunatic tourist, set out to rescue him. After catching up with Gill on the upper reaches of the mountain and talking things over, the guide, says Gill, "decided that I wasn't as big a nut as he had assumed I was from below, and we continued on to the top together." Other similarly exciting climbs followed, and by the end of the summer Gill knew he had found his calling.

The following fall, while a freshman at Georgia Tech, Gill was required to take a gymnastics course. The class was shown a film of Olympic gymnasts performing on the still rings, and Gill, never having seen the sport before, was "amazed at the poise with which those gymnasts accomplished their routines. They did enormously difficult things while appearing to be very relaxed and controlled." The film made a strong impression on him; it was epiphanic. Wasn't rock climbing, Gill mused, really nothing more than a kind of free-form gymnastics? Immediately, he began to use the tools of gymnastics—the scientific training regimen, the mental discipline, powdered chalk for the hands to enhance grip—to assault the traditional bounds of mountaineering.

Gill combed the hill country of Georgia and Alabama looking for crags to climb. There being a dearth of large cliffs to scale in these states, he naturally turned his attention to small outcrops and boulders. To keep from becoming bored, he used his newly acquired gymnastic skills to milk every last drop of challenge from his miniature alps. And thus was the sport of bouldering born. (Mountaineers had been practicing on boulders long before Gill appeared, but they generally regarded bouldering as nothing more than a training adjunct for "real" mountain climbing; Gill was the first person to pursue boulder climbing as a worthwhile end in itself.)

During his college years Gill often spent his summer vacations in the Tetons and other corners of the Rockies. On his first trips to the West he did climb a number of major peaks such as the Grand Teton, but he found himself devoting more of his attention to smaller and smaller (and harder and harder) pieces of rock. In Pat Ament's *Master of Rock*, a monograph about Gill, Yvon Chouinard recalls the days he and Gill shared in the Tetons in the late 1950s. According to Chouinard, Gill was one of a handful of eccentric climbers who resided in the Tetons during the summer months, living to climb, "scrounging on fifty cents a day, eating oatmeal." Gill had by then taken to eschewing summits, says Chouinard, and was "doing things just for the sake of pure climbing, going nowhere. These were absurd climbs as far as the American Alpine Club was concerned."

Before long, Gill gave up conventional roped climbing altogether and concentrated solely on climbing low boulders of extraordinary difficulty, in solitude, a practice that caused him to suffer no small amount of derision from tradition-bound climbers. Among those who paid Gill any heed at all, it was widely assumed that he had lost his nerve and become too acrophobic to climb more than twenty feet off the deck. In reality Gill was on an intense personal quest —poking and probing at the limits of gravity, stone, muscle, and mind to see where, beyond topographical heights, climbing might lead him.

The sport of mountain climbing is notably lacking in formal governing bodies and official rules. In spite of this—or perhaps because of this—the tight-knit community of established American climbers has always projected a very strong sense of how the game ought to be played, and an insidious kind of peer pressure is exerted to persuade climbers to conform to this sense.

"As early as 1957," Gill notes, "I recognized that mainstream philosophy is a very binding force that can keep you locked into a certain perspective, and I didn't like that. Most of all, I like the freedom of climbing. I grew up in the Deep South, where you're surrounded by thick, soft trees, and it's hard to see the sky because of the humidity. The landscape, by and large, is flat. Nature doesn't confront you there. It was a tremendous transition for me to come

△ 19

out West for the first time. I was overwhelmed by the rocks, by the scale, by the wide-open space. The marvelous thing about climbing to me, having grown up in a rather cloistered existence, was the exhilaration of being out in this natural state, where there were these great environmental challenges and all this freedom to maneuver.

"When I first recognized the tremendous force of a mainstream perspective," Gill continues, "the tremendous force that a climbing community can exert upon your climbing experience, I realized that I wanted to experiment with climbing, that I wasn't interested in making my climbing fall into a category, walking in someone else's footsteps, or obeying a set of informal rules, even if unwritten rules. I decided that an easy way to avoid the restrictive mainstream perspective was to climb in solitude. I simply found it to be very, very difficult to experiment while climbing with other people, or even while staying at a climbers' campground. When I climbed in solitude I discovered that I had marvelous inner adventures."

These days, it's not unusual to see teenagers who once would have spent their free time on a softball field or basketball court instead grab rock shoes and chalk bags and make for the boulders. Thanks to the activity's accessibility, uncomplicated format, and instant intensity, bouldering is currently very much in vogue. It's easy to forget that Gill was alone in bucking a powerful tide when he specialized in minimalist climbing three decades ago. Now he warns other boulderers that they should be wary of getting overly caught up in the established practices of bouldering; he continually urges would-be rock stars to look for direction from within.

In an article titled "Notes on Bouldering—The Vertical Path," Gill wrote,

> Continually question climbing pursuits. Do they draw one
> back to the climbing community? Or do they lead along the
> [inner-directed] path? This questioning generates a tension that
> is heightened by disillusionment. Ultimately, one reaches an

emptiness, and this is where our basic spontaneous nature leads
to the beginning of the path . . . Thereafter one can
continually stand apart from the outer world of climbing, yet
at times be fiercely involved in it. Philosophical and mystical
dimensions emerge when the two worlds are brought together.

At times Gill's prose can be as dense and recondite as one of his
mathematical proofs, but it rings clear and true to those who share
his obsession with vertical ground. It's not unusual to hear buzz-
cut adolescent rock prodigies quoting Gill verbatim from one of
the articles about bouldering he's written for mountaineering jour-
nals. The gentlemanly middle-aged mathematics scholar has become a guru of the boulder fields, a role model for a generation of
young men and women who dress in chartreuse tights, sport gold
studs in their nostrils, and climb with the apocalyptic rhythms of
Jane's Addiction or the Fine Young Cannibals rumbling through
the headphones of their Walkmen.

No one, it is worth pointing out, would have paid any attention
to Gill or his innovative ideas if he had simply been a boulderer,
and not a brilliant boulderer. Gill is regarded as a hero instead of
a crank because on occasion he has stepped off his private mystical
path and become "fiercely involved" in the conventional climbing
paradigm, where he has demonstrated that he can play the game
according to the traditional rules as well as anyone ever has.

Climbing can be a ruthlessly competitive sport. The lack of formal competitive outlets makes it hard to establish a precise hierarchy
of ascensionists, but a surprisingly accurate, if arcane, system for
rating the difficulty of rock climbs was developed in Southern California in the 1950s that gives climbers some sense of how they
stack up. The method is called the Yosemite Decimal System, and
it rates the difficulty of technical climbs on a scale that originally
ran from 5.0 to 5.9.

Within a few years of starting to climb, Gill was pioneering
conventional roped climbs of 5.9 difficulty, the top of the scale, on
Disappointment Peak and other Teton cliffs. At the end of the

1950s, when he began to really concentrate on bouldering, almost all of the problems he "put up" were much too hard to even register on the existing YDS scale. Gill was climbing at a 5.12 standard a good twenty years before such a rating came into existence (The standards in climbing, as in other athletic activities, have been raised considerably in the last thirty years: The 5.10 rating was added to the scale in the sixties; the 5.11 rating in the seventies; 5.12, 5.13, and 5.14 ratings thus far in the eighties).

In 1961, Gill put up a boulder problem that is still talked about in hushed tones: the north face of the Thimble, a thirty-foot over-hanging spire in the Needles of South Dakota. Gill's route on the Thimble demands everything an ultimate boulder problem should—unlikely sequences of simultaneously delicate and stren-uous moves on fingertip holds—and more: The climb is positioned directly above a parking-lot guardrail, and a fall from high up would likely result in death, or worse. At the time of this writing, nearly thirty years later, Gill's ropeless ascent of the problem has yet to be repeated.

Gill isn't entirely sure what moved him to climb the Thimble. The rock formation, he says, "was aesthetic and very clean. There were very few holds on it. I was a lot less concerned with safety in those days than I am now. Nowadays I'll put a rope on to cross the street or step off the curb. I felt as though I had to do something with an element of risk in it, something difficult."

After looking the climb over very carefully and determining "what sorts of moves I would be responsible for, if I were willing to commit myself to the climb," Gill trained for an entire winter in the gym at the Air Force base in Montana where he was then stationed. "I did squeeze-type exercises," he says, "because I no-ticed there were some little nubbins up there that I would have to squeeze when the horizontal holds ran out. They run out pretty fast. I devised little climbs on nuts and bolts sticking out of the wall of the gymnasium. I would squeeze the bolts and pull myself up. The Thimble was on my mind for much of that winter."

△ 22

The following spring, Gill returned to the Black Hills, where the Needles are located, to attempt the climb. He climbed up and down the lower half of the rock over and over, memorizing the moves and building confidence, "getting it wired." He says that "going up and down, up and down, eventually I worked myself into such a fevered pitch that I committed myself to the top portion and very fortunately made it. It's like a lot of other sporting activities. You not only get psyched up but almost become hypnotized or mesmerized to the point where your mind goes blank, and you climb by well-cultivated instinct."

Climbing the Thimble marked a turning point in Gill's life. Soon after that he got married and stopped doing climbs that he considered risky. "I think risk can be addictive," he explains, "and I didn't want to become addicted. The intensity not only increases but changes in character when you climb things that you simply cannot afford to fall off of. It's difficult to put into words, but I found myself going into almost a different state of consciousness when I was climbing unroped in a dangerous situation. My limbs became very light, my breathing altered very subtly, and I'm sure there were vascular changes that I wasn't really aware of at the time. I noticed that I went into this different physiological configuration on life-threatening climbs. It was exhilarating and very intense, but almost in a relaxed way. There might be gripping moments, but there would still be this thread of relaxation throughout the whole climb. It was fascinating, but I didn't want to get hooked on it."

That Gill was so much better than the other rock climbers of the day can be attributed to his experimental, open-minded approach. He trained intensively on gymnastic apparatus when he wasn't on the rocks, building strength to the point where he could chin himself while hanging from a single finger. A longtime student of Zen, he prepared his mind as thoroughly as he prepared his musculature. He had an affinity for meditation, and found that by focusing all his attention on, say, a blade of grass or a mountain landscape before a climb, it would clear his mind, prime his body, and give him the calm assurance necessary to get him over sketchy terrain. To Gill, maintaining an inner calm during moments of extreme stress is one of the ultimate goals in climbing. "When you reach such an advanced state of technical skill that you don't really notice exertion," he explains, "only then do you really begin to feel the climbing. You'll never feel the joy of movement if you're struggling. You've got to get good enough and strong enough to reach the point where you can feel this quintessential lightness. It's an illusion of course, but it's nice to be able to dwell upon that illusion. I don't feel as though I'm entirely successful on a boulder problem if I don't achieve that feeling of lightness."

Although at fifty-four Gill can still make it up a few boulder problems that repel "totally honed" twenty-two-year-old rock jocks, in the last twenty years he has increasingly been seeking out other things besides pure difficulty in his bouldering, trying, as he puts it, "to find ways of getting more and more out of less and less." His reputation for never climbing higher than thirty feet to the contrary, Gill does in fact regularly ascend—alone and without a rope—what he considers to be easy routes on eight-hundred-foot-high cliffs near his home, as an exercise in "kinesthetic meditation."

"I think I've had some interesting experiences," he says, "because I've 'over-trained,' in a sense, for some of these long, easy climbs that I do over and over again. I have these routes wired to such a degree that I don't have to think about the climbing on a conscious level. I become so involved with the flow and the pattern of the climb that I lose touch with who I am and what I am and become part of the rock—I've actually felt at times as though I was weaving in and out of the rock."

"I don't know how much of this I should talk about," Gill says hesitantly in his soft baritone, "because I don't want people to think I've wigged out, but I believe that all the years of mental and physical preparation that I went through in developing both my climbing and mathematical skills—concentrating for long periods of time on a single crystal of rock or getting very deeply into a difficult mathematical problem—made it very easy for me to have certain kinds of mystical experiences.

"In the mid 1970s," Gill elaborates, "a good friend of mine became very interested in Carlos Casteneda's books and kept trying to get me to read them. I've never taken hallucinatory drugs and have no interest in drugs, and I resisted reading these books because I thought they were all about drugs. But my friend finally convinced me that this wasn't the case, and I read them and found them to be fascinating. It may be in his second book—I'm not certain—his central character describes the procedure for initiating himself into the art of dreaming. That so intrigued me that I decided to try it. And I had *instant* success!

"There are various stages in this dream state or hypnogogic state, this alternate reality. You are entirely conscious, almost more conscious than you are in a regular waking state. Sometimes you can go floating over a city, do that sort of thing, but at other times it's very much like our normal mode of existence where the normal rules of gravitation apply; you're just somewhere else.

"I've found that the easiest time for me to capture this hypnogogic state is during the middle of the night, when I awaken and then slowly drift back to sleep, but I have also entered a similar state while climbing, particularly when soloing those long, easy routes —those times when I feel as though I'm being sewn into the rock. I can come closest then to this second reality, this feeling of lightness. And that, really, is the transcendental poetry of climbing. I consider experiencing that hypnogogic state to be far more important than being able to climb extremely difficult boulder problems that nobody has climbed."

Lately, Gill has become more fascinated than ever with the metaphysical side of bouldering, the inner climbing experience. Once, after drinking a bit of wine, Gill speculated about the possibility that "an excellent mental attitude" may induce a telekinetic ability to levitate, if only slightly. "A few ounces could make a tremendous

difference," he muses. "I have seen people go beyond their limits."
Hundreds, maybe thousands, of expert climbers have toiled for
uncountable hours at the bases of John Gill's boulder problems,
trying in vain to get both their feet off the ground. Many of these
climbers might ordinarily be inclined to scoff when talk turns to
telekinesis and the like, but when Gill talks about levitation, they
listen very, very carefully.

3. VALDEZ ICE

VALDEZ, ALASKA, IS A SMALL TOWN WITH TWO BIG CLAIMS TO FAME. The first is that on Good Friday, 1964, this community of four thousand souls, tucked between the foot of the Chugach Mountains and a narrow arm of the sea, was rocked by the most powerful earthquake ever recorded in North America, a catastrophe that killed thirty-three residents. The second, of course, is that Valdez (pronounced val-DEEZ) was also the site of North America's biggest, most environmentally catastrophic oil spill: more than ten million gallons of heavy North Slope crude.

The spilling of all that oil in 1989 is attributable to complacency, corporate greed, a captain's fondness for demon drink, and Murphy's immutable Law; that the oil spilled into Valdez Arm, and not some other body of water, is attributable to a quirk of climate: the trans-Alaska pipeline goes to Valdez, and thus supertankers like the Exxon *Valdez* go to Valdez, because Valdez is the northernmost ice-free port on the continent.

If the waters of Valdez Arm are free of ice year-round, however, the land that surrounds them is anything but. The fat blue tongues of several glaciers thrust well into the Valdez city limits, and throughout the winter months frigid temperatures and the damp marine air conspire to glaze the downtown streets with a treacherous armor of black ice. But the most impressive ice formations are found on the lower flanks of the mile-high peaks that bristle like shark's teeth, in row after jagged row, just beyond the edge of town.

In summer hundreds of waterfalls pour off these rain-drenched escarpments; come November the falls freeze solid in mid-cascade, their tumbling mists transmogrified by the winter's cold into icicles the size of skyscrapers—towering pillars and bizarre curtains of fragile-looking ice that glow in pale shades of aquamarine and sapphire in the low subarctic light.

About fifteen miles from the center of metropolitan Valdez, the sole highway out of town enters Keystone Canyon: a narrow, eight-hundred-foot-deep gash across the hard-rock spine of the Chugach Range, through which the Lowe River rushes to the sea. Although the canyon is only two and a half miles from end to end, in the winter more than fifty frozen waterfalls hang from its vertical and overhanging walls.

Ten years ago, a Valdez ship's agent named Bob Pudwill was driving through Keystone Canyon beneath these forbidding cliffs when, he recalls, "I happened to look up and see a tiny figure standing on a ledge halfway up Bridal Veil Falls," one of the canyon's largest cascades, which, from November until May, turns into a fifty-story-high latticework of delicate blue icicles. The figure on the falls, Pudwill explains, was "stamping his feet and slapping his hands together while paying out a line which ran up to a second tiny figure who appeared to be stuck to the ice, spread-eagled who knows how, let alone why. My only guess was that they must be getting paid."

In fact they were not getting paid, nor, as Pudwill alternately suspected, were they attempting a novel form of suicide; the two people were climbing the waterfall, in a certain historical sense, because it was there: The activity Pudwill witnessed, lunatic though it appeared to be, was nothing less than the latest eminently logical refinement of the venerable sport of mountaineering. Within a year Mr. Pudwill was an ardent waterfall climber himself.

When mountain climbing was invented in the Alps two hundred years ago, it was an admirably simple sport: One found oneself a mountain, the bigger the better, and tried to climb to its top. By and by, however, all the highest summits were reached, and alpinists who wanted to make a mark for themselves were forced to

△ 28

turn to increasingly difficult faces and ridges on peaks that had already been climbed. Eventually the quest for ever greater challenges and virgin vertical ground evolved to the point where, for a good many climbers, reaching a geographically significant summit ceased to be of any interest whatsoever; so long as the climbing was hard enough and steep enough to make adrenaline flow in abundance, it was unimportant whether the object being climbed was a high Himalayan peak or an English rock quarry. Or, indeed, a frozen waterfall in Valdez, Alaska.

A Valdez waterfall known as Wowie Zowie happened to be the objective of John Weiland and Bob Shelton on January 25, 1987. Being that Wowie Zowie plunges from the lip of an overhanging cliff in a single, unbroken, four-hundred-foot drop, and their three-eighths-inch diameter climbing rope was three hundred feet long, the climbers planned to attack the giant icicle in two stages—or "pitches," in the lexicon of ascent—the first of which would end two hundred feet up, at a small hollow in the back of the ice flow.

Shelton started up the first pitch at 9 A.M. In each hand he held an ice axe (a thin six-inch steel pick attached to a sixteen-inch fiberglass handle), and strapped to the soles of his climbing boots were crampons (sets of two-inch steel spikes, twelve per boot, two of which pointed forward from the toe of each foot). By planting the picks of his ice axes with a series of carefully directed swings, and balancing on the toe spikes of his crampons after kicking them half an inch into the ice, Shelton hauled himself up the sheer face of Wowie Zowie like an overgrown arachnid, a technique known as front-pointing.

To safeguard his ascent as much as possible, every twenty or thirty feet Shelton would pause to twist in an ice screw (a threaded eight-inch aluminum or titanium tube with an eye at one end), clip a carabiner (an aluminum snap-link) through the eye of the screw, and then clip the rope trailing from his waist harness through the carabiner.

By this system, if he were to lose his tenuous attachment to the ice while he was, say, fifteen feet above a screw placement, Shelton could expect to fall about forty feet before his downward flight was arrested by Weiland's belay (belaying being a method of paying out rope in a fashion that permits it to be anchored instantaneously in the event of a fall): Shelton would drop the fifteen feet back down to the screw, another fifteen feet past it, as well as an additional ten feet or so as the rope stretched to absorb the force of the fall. Since falling forty feet with working replicas of the weapon that was used to assassinate Trotsky windmilling about one's person could conceivably do some serious damage, Shelton was trying very hard to heed the adage "the leader must not fall."

A hundred feet off the ground, after two arm-withering hours of battling gravity and the brittle ice of Wowie Zowie, Shelton reached an overlap in the giant icicle, a point where the pillar above overhung his position like a ragged, rotting awning. "I scrunched up under the overhang as tight as I could," Shelton remembers, "and fired in another screw. Then I leaned out past the lip of the roof, got my axes planted on the face of the pillar, yelled down for Johnny to watch my ass, and went for it: I swung out on my arms, cranked off a pull-up, and started front-pointing on up the pillar."

Much to Shelton's dismay, he discovered that the ice of the dead-vertical upper pillar was an infirm concoction honeycombed with air pockets, resembling flimsy Styrofoam more than ice. Climbing back down the overhang he'd just surmounted, however, was impossible, so he pushed onward, hoping the condition of the ice would improve as he got higher. Instead, it got worse. As he swung his ice axes over and over with burning arms, trying in vain to chop through the bad ice to find something solid to sink his picks into, he found it harder and harder to keep a grip on the tools. Then, says Shelton, "all of a sudden everything kind of sheared out on me, and I peeled."

"Peel," "catch some air," "take a screamer," "log some flight time"; such are the quaint turns of phrase climbers use to denote the act of falling. In Shelton's case, when he hurtled upside down past the lip of the overhang and the force of the fall plucked his uppermost screw out of the rotten ice like a toothpick from a canape, it began to look like he might actually "crater," a verb reserved for occasions when a climber suffers the misfortune of falling all the way to the ground. Luck, however, was on Shelton's side that Sunday, for the next screw held, and he bounced to a stop on the stretchy nylon rope after falling a mere sixty feet, bruised but otherwise unharmed.

Frozen waterfalls like Wowie Zowie, it should be pointed out, are a fairly new addition to the list of things climbers climb, for the simple reason that until the late 1960s nobody had the means to climb them. Alpinists, to be sure, have been ascending icy faces and gullies since mountaineering's earliest days, but only when the inclines involved were considerably less than vertical.

By the nineteenth century, climbers shod in hobnailed boots were dispatching ice faces as steep as forty or fifty degrees on Mont Blanc and the neighboring *Aiguilles* by laboriously hewing long lines of steps and handholds up the slopes with crude, heavy ice axes. In 1908, the upper limit of steepness was pushed a few more degrees toward vertical with the invention, by an English climber named Oscar Eckenstein, of a crampon sporting ten downward-pointing spikes.

By the 1930s, the crampon had sprouted the additional pair of spikes protruding horizontally at the toe, and by the mid-1960s teeth had been notched into the pick-end of the ice axe. With these refinements climbers were able to develop the audacious technique of front-pointing, obviating altogether the need to chop steps, and allowing the leading climbers of the day to claw their way up ice gullies as steep as seventy degrees in the French Alps, the Scottish Highlands, and the Rocky Mountains of North America.

Unfortunately, when climbers tried to push the edge of the envelope further still, they found that their tools were woefully inadequate for the task. On ice steeper than seventy degrees, explains

Yvon Chouinard, a compact Californian of French-Canadian descent who was perhaps the premiere ice climber of the 1960s, "even the best ice axes tended to pop out of the ice and hit you in the eye when they were called upon to support much body weight."

Chouinard, a self-taught blacksmith, eked out a living in those days selling state-of-the-art pitons, carabiners, and other climbing paraphernalia of his own innovative design and manufacture. In 1966, after becoming frustrated with the shortcomings of the tools he had used to ascend some of the great ice faces of the Mont Blanc massif, Chouinard resolved to try and come up with something better: an ice axe, specifically, that could be relied upon to stick securely in vertical ice. "On a rainy day that summer," he remembers, "I went out on the Bossons Glacier, above Chamonix, to test every ice axe then available, to try and figure out why they didn't work."

One thing he immediately noticed was that all the ice axes he tested had been forged with straight picks that were aligned perpendicular to their handles. On a hunch, Chouinard—with the assistance of a climbing partner named Tom Frost, an aeronautical engineer—designed an ice axe with a pick that hooked downward in a gentle curve that matched the arc of the axe as it was swung.

The hunch proved to be a stroke of genius: Armed with a Chouinard-Frost ice axe in each hand, a climber with strong arms and a stout heart could front-point his way up vertical and even overhanging ice. In 1970 the Chouinard-Frost ice axe became available in climbing shops worldwide, launching a string of previously unthinkable ascents of surreal, behemoth icicles from Alaska to Kenya and New Hampshire to Norway, more than a few of which were first climbed by Chouinard himself.

From the late 1950s through the late 1960s, when Chouinard was in his twenties and first developing a reputation as an inventor of extraordinary climbing equipment, he spent much of each year on the road traveling from climbing area to climbing area with a portable coal-fired forge, he says, "just climbing and selling gear I'd make out of the trunk of my car." His income was often meager at best during this period. Frequently his finances were stretched so thin that he and his climbing partners would be forced to subsist on ground squirrels and porcupines, although in relatively flush times, Chouinard recalls, "we'd splurge and buy damaged cans of cat food. We'd get them for a dime apiece, and stock up for the entire summer." Lest anyone get the wrong impression, Chouinard is quick to add that "it was the fancy kind of cat food, the tuna flavored stuff. I mean, I'm not the kind of person who would eat *dog* food or anything."

Chouinard, now fifty-one years old, is still climbing at a high standard and still making what are widely regarded as the world's finest ice-climbing tools, but these days it's safe to assume that he no longer eats a lot of pet food, even of the fancy feline variety, because the equipment company he started in 1957 from the back of a decrepit Ford has mushroomed into a family of related businesses that take in more than $70 million a year.

The bulk of these revenues come not from sales of ice screws and ice axes and crampons, but from a line of stylish, ingeniously designed outdoor clothing—parkas, rain gear, long underwear, and the like—marketed under the Patagonia label. Chouinard, in fact, says he's never made any money from ice-climbing hardware and never expects to, because ice climbing is such a cold, strange, scary activity that the market for the equipment will always remain extremely limited. Indeed, of the estimated 150,000 Americans who would call themselves serious mountaineers, at most one per cent of them climb frozen waterfalls on a regular basis. "Pretty much the only people who ice-climb," the master ice climber declares matter-of-factly, "are a handful of maladjusted geeks."

Not surprisingly, a disproportionate number of these maladjusted geeks live in or near Valdez, Alaska. Some of the Valdez ice climbers, like Dr. Andrew Embick, one of the town's three physicians, were hard-core climbing fanatics from the lower forty-eight who emigrated to the area, at least in part, specifically to take advantage of its icy munificence; others were ordinary nonclimbing residents who had no idea when they arrived in the region that a bizarre sport like waterfall climbing even existed, let alone that they would one day take it up themselves.

Ice climbing can be a seductive pastime. When John Weiland— who introduced waterfall climbing to Valdez in 1975—speaks about his early climbing experiences, you have to remind yourself that he is talking about a sport, not a form of substance abuse. "My father was an obsessed climber," the thoughtful forty-one-year-old carpenter reports, "so I was exposed to it at an early age, and got completely hooked on the sport, too. Climbing was like a drug to me, it was everything."

In 1976, not long after he and visiting Coloradan Jeff Lowe completed the three-day first ascent of Keystone Green Steps, at 650 feet the biggest waterfall in Valdez, Weiland began to resent the way his magnificent obsession was monopolizing his life. He forced himself to quit climbing, cold turkey, and managed to remain on the wagon for nearly six full years. In 1981, however, in a weak moment he dusted off his ice tools and did a little climbing, just to prove to himself that he could take it or leave it, and has been back fooling around on frozen waterfalls ever since. Weiland soberly insists, however, that he "got back into it real slowly, and I've been careful not to go crazy with it this time around. I feel like I'm in control now."

Addiction, of course, is not the only hazard confronting the ice climber. The activity is so unmistakably dangerous, however, that it tends to scare away people who don't know what they're doing before they can get far enough off the ground to kill themselves. Thus far, at any rate, there have been surprisingly few ice-climbing accidents in Valdez, and none that were fatal. "Certainly," Andy Embick points out, "ice climbing is not a completely benign sport, but in Valdez, over the course of nine years of aggressive waterfall climbing, we've seen only eight or nine injuries, the most serious being a couple of broken legs."

△ 34

Dr. Embick—a manic, muscular, Harvard-educated family practitioner in his early forties who wears wire-rim glasses and an Abraham Lincoln beard—is so bullish on ice climbing that he has been known to prescribe it to patients as a form of preventive medicine. "Alaskans," he explains, "tend not to do well in the winter. Many are unemployed for the entire season, and the paucity of available activities, the short days, the lousy weather, all lead them to spend a lot of time cooped up indoors. One effect is that we have a big baby boom every October; the other is that people sit around, get unhappy, drink way too much, beat their husbands or wives. The darkness does evil things to the mind, resulting in one or two suicides every year. Anything that gets you out, that gets you physically active, is going to be good psychotherapy and stave off winter problems. And ice climbing is one of the few physical outlets available to people here in the winter."

The fact that few of Embick's patients have actually been persuaded to take this particular cure seems to quell the good doctor's passion for his slippery pastime not a whit. It's a passion that is made manifest in many ways, not least of which is "The Book," a magnum opus Embick has been compiling for the past nine years, which, if ever published, will bear the title *Blue Ice and Black Gold: An Ice Climber's Guide to the Frozen Waterfalls of Valdez, Alaska.* In addition to describing each of the 164 waterfalls that have thus far been climbed, The Book lists the names of the first ascensionists (Embick's own name appears alongside fifty of the climbs) and grades the difficulty of every waterfall on a scale of I to VI.

Although ice climbing is a game played without benefit of referees, official rules, or organized competitions, it's intensely competitive all the same. The best ice climbers, who train with the dedication of Olympic athletes, rely on The Book and similar guides not so much as Baedekers, but rather as a handy means for establishing a pecking order: A person who has climbed a waterfall rated Grade VI in The Book plainly has more bragging rights than a person who has climbed one rated Grade V + .

Special prestige, obviously, is attached to making first ascents. Not only are those who first subdue a given waterfall immortalized in The Book, but they earn the right to name the cascade as they see fit. A quick glance through The Book's pages reveals that the local taste in waterfall names runs to such creative handles as Killer Death Fang Falls, Deo Gratias, Never Again, Necromancer, Thrash & Bash, Too Loose Lautrec, No Way Jose, Dire Straits, and Marginal Desperation. A number of the appellations, not fit to print, are inspired by bodily functions and adolescent sexual fixations, reflecting the arrested development of the typical ice climber.

In the interest of promoting waterfall climbing in general and Valdez waterfall climbing in particular, in February, 1983, Embick staged the first annual Valdez Ice Climbing Festival, a loosely structured opportunity for local climbers to schmooze and drink beer and climb with their out-of-town brethren. The community has continued to host the event every February since. In past years, the festival has drawn ice climbers from places as far afield as Austria, New Zealand, Japan, and Kentucky.

To ensure that out-of-town climbers have a memorable visit, the Valdez climbers like to point their guests toward the "really classic" waterfalls in town. In 1985, for instance, a local ace named Brian Teale guided Shomo Suzuki—perhaps Japan's finest ice climber—up Wowie Zowie, which at the time was so classic that it had been climbed only once since its first ascent in 1981 by Embick and a brilliant Fairbanks climber named Carl Tobin. If Suzuki had had a chance to study The Book he would have found the waterfall described as "a striking, overhanging pillar," with ice of "very poor consistency," and a long section on which "the chance of stopping or retreating was impossible." After the climb, when asked how Wowie Zowie stacked up against the waterfalls on his home turf, Suzuki reportedly replied without hesitation, "No ice like this has ever been climbed in Japan, and I, for one, have no intention of ever climbing any again."

△ 36

In 1987 I came to Valdez for the Ice Festival and found sixty-three other climbers in attendance, forty of whom bivouacked each night, cheek by jowl, on Embick's floor. I also found that my hosts, with the same hospitality they extended toward Mr. Suzuki, went out of their way to see that I had a memorable stay. During the week I spent in Alaska I was taken to climb eight local classics, the most classic of all being a waterfall with the innocuous-sounding name of Love's Way.

The 360-foot waterfall had first been climbed in 1980 by Embick and Tobin—Embick christened it Love's Way to commemorate his impending marriage—and had not seen a repeat ascent until two months before my arrival. After agreeing to accompany a brash young Fairbanks climber named Roman Dial on an attempt of the climb, I read in The Book with growing anxiety that Love's Way consists "of an overhanging, candle-sticked, free-hanging pillar separated from the rock . . . As is typical of overhanging ice, placements for both tools and screws are poor at best." The passage then went on to warn that "pure power and endurance" would not be sufficient in themselves to bring about success; that in addition it would be necessary to execute "complex stemming, jamming, and laybacking on fragile icicles"—sophisticated techniques borrowed from the technical rock climber's repertoire.

Climbers attacking a difficult ice climb will typically do so as a team of two. In keeping with the gregarious spirit of the Ice Festival, however, Roman and I were joined on Love's Way by Kate Bull, a twenty-seven-year-old geologist, and Brian Teale. Love's Way was intersected by two large ledges, breaking the climb into three logical pitches. Both Brian and Roman, like most hard-core climbers, are notorious "lead hogs": They regard climbing second or third on the rope with the protection of a belay from above to be as unfulfilling as playing poker without betting real money, and are consequently loath to relinquish the so-called sharp end of the rope.

After a long discussion it was agreed that Brian would tie in to the sharp end for the first pitch. It proved to be of only moderate difficulty, and he front-pointed rapidly up to the ledge at its top, where he placed three ice screws, tied himself to these anchors, and proceeded to belay Kate, Roman, and me up to the ledge in turn. Directly above us, looming like Damocles's sword, was the crux second pitch of the climb: a twelve-story-high pillar, the first seven stories of it being a top-heavy free-standing bundle of fragile-looking icicles, the lot of them no bigger around at the pillar's base than the trunk of a small tree.

At this point, following a close examination of the pillar, it seemed that much of the passion had gone out of the two lead hogs' protestations about who deserved the honor of leading the second pitch. In fact, when Brian unexpectedly offered, "Yeah, Roman, if you really want to lead it that bad, I guess I'll let you," for an instant I thought I detected a few cracks in Roman's usually fearless demeanor. His hesitation might have had something to do with an incident the month before, when he had watched a partner named Chuck Comstock come within inches of getting lunched on a disturbingly similar free-standing pillar in the nearby Wrangell Range.

Comstock, a redheaded Iowa farm boy who had never heard of ice climbing until he joined the Coast Guard and was shipped off to Valdez, had been leading the pillar in question, the final pitch of a fifteen-hundred-foot waterfall, when the giant icicle he was front-pointing began to creak and groan ominously. When the creaking suddenly began to increase in volume, Comstock finally abandoned his lead and beat a panicked retreat. A few seconds after he reached the pillar's base and scurried aside, the pillar collapsed of its own immense, ill-supported weight with a thunderous roar while Roman looked on in disbelief.

With his friend's close shave no doubt still fresh in his mind, Roman swung his ice tools into the second pitch of Love's Way as gingerly as a gem cutter cleaving a priceless stone. Upward progress called for a paradoxical blend of power and great delicacy; the climbing was unrelentingly tenuous. The ice on the pillar was so brittle and insubstantial that Roman didn't waste his time trying to protect himself with any ice screws until he was a good forty feet above the belay ledge, and when he did finally place one the ice surrounding it was so poor that the vibration from his rope wiggled the screw right out of the ice as he climbed above the placement.

Roman wasn't able to place a reliable ice screw until he was eighty feet above the belay ledge. Had he experienced a failing of strength or made a single mistake before placing that screw— if his tools, for instance, had sheared out of the ice like Bob Shelton's had on Wowie Zowie—in all likelihood Roman would have fallen to his death. Most people in his shoes would have been quite literally paralyzed with fear, which only would have hastened their demise. In Roman's case, however, the seriousness of the situation simply served to sharpen his concentration and dull the fatigue in his arms, and he reached the ledge at the top of the second pitch without incident, albeit utterly spent both mentally and physically.

It was my turn next. After the cramps in his arms had subsided, Roman pulled up the slack in the rope and yelled down, "You're on belay!" my cue to step up to the pillar and have at it. The well-anchored rope from above meant that I had nothing to worry about as long as I didn't inadvertently chop through my lifeline with an ice axe or knock down the pillar, so I aimed my ice axes with care, and swung them as lightly as possible. Even so, every time I planted an axe or kicked in a crampon the whole pillar resonated with a loud *THUNK!* and shook disconcertingly underfoot, making me feel as though I were up a tree that was being chopped down.

I tried to steer clear of gray, funky, rotten ice, aiming my picks only at spots where the pillar was a deep blue-green, and hence relatively sturdy. But even the green ice was permeated with hidden voids and air pockets, making it impossible to get the tools to stick

△ 39

solidly. And no matter how carefully I swung my axes, every so often a shard of ice—some weighing twenty or thirty pounds—would break off beneath my blows, brush past my head, accelerate earthward with a low whistle, and smash into the slope twenty stories below as I looked on, transfixed.

Due to the lamentable diameter of the pillar, I was forced to plant my crampons close together in an awkward, pigeon-toed posture, making it difficult to remain in balance: Each time I'd pull, say, my left pick out of the ice to plant it higher, the left side of my body would swing crazily away from the overhanging pillar, like the door of a cupboard that's been installed out of plumb and won't stay shut.

Because the ice was overhanging, my arms were called upon to support approximately eighty percent of my body weight for most of the thirty or forty minutes it took to ascend the pillar. The physical effort was roughly comparable to doing pull-ups from a chinning bar for half an hour straight, pausing at the top of each pull-up to hang from one arm and swing a two-pound hammer a couple of times with the other. By the time I was halfway up the second pitch of Love's Way my arms were quivering from the strain, I was gasping for air, and—despite the cold—the clothing beneath my wind suit was soaked with sweat; by the time I finally flopped down onto the ledge where Roman was belaying, my hands were cramping so badly I could barely squeeze open the gate of a carabiner.

Kate came up next, then Brian, and just before sunset the four of us nervously turned our attention to the final pitch still above us. To everyone's relief, it turned out to be merely vertical as opposed to overhanging—it was a cruise compared to the pillar—and as the evening's bitter chill settled on Valdez, our motley team shook hands beside the clump of stunted alders that marked the summit of Love's Way.

There is no denying that waterfall climbing is usually scary, sometimes miserable, occasionally even genuinely life-threatening.

△ 40

Most nonclimbers, try as they might, have trouble fathoming the sport's appeal. Anyone who had heard Kate Bull's exultant whoops echo from the walls of Keystone Canyon as she pulled up onto the top of Love's Way would have had absolutely no trouble at all.

4. ON BEING TENTBOUND

THE NEXT TIME YOU'RE PLANNING A TRIP TO THE BACKCOUNTRY, YOUR enthusiasm sparked by some glossy coffee-table book picturing snowcapped peaks under perfect blue skies, you would do well to keep in mind whence that glorious snowpack came. It is the nature of mountains to wring from the winds what moisture they happen to be carrying. This you already know, of course, if not from high school science classes, then from sodden vacations in the Adirondacks and the North Cascades. But optimism is dangerously immune to simple facts and the hard lessons of experience. It can be difficult to admit that spending time in the unspoiled wilds, more often than not, means doing time within the walls of a dank nylon cell, tentbound.

Some mountains and seasons, of course, produce nastier weather than others, and by steering clear of places like the Himalaya during the monsoon or Patagonia (where, as the locals say, "the wind sweeps the land like the broom of God") any time of the year, you are likely to occasionally encounter fair skies. But mosquitoes and blackflies can confine you to the tent under the brightest sun, as can desert sandstorms, so becoming tentbound is always a possibility, no matter what the weather report.

It is true that when tent life gets old in the lesser ranges, at least in the summer, you can usually don clammy rain gear and venture outside in spite of the deluge to glean what pleasure you can from the misty hills. But if you're ever seduced by the wilder and more dramatic charms of some remote, glaciated, major league range, you risk finding yourself incarcerated in a tent, a hostage of the elements, for days and perhaps weeks at a time.

Being tentbound isn't wholly an ordeal. The first few hours can pass in a dreamy euphoria while you lie peacefully in your sleeping bag, watching raindrops trickle down the outside of the translucent fly, or the snowdrifts slowly climb the walls. Wrapped snugly in down or the latest achievement of the chemical industry, with the daylight's cruel condition filtered by nylon into a soothing twilight, there is an atmosphere of guiltless relief. The tempest has blessed you with a sturdy alibi for not risking your life attempting the first free *direttissima* of that frightening pinnacle up the valley or laboring over yet another high pass as part of your partner's absurd plan to explore the next watershed to the east. Your life is secure for at least another day; needless toil has been averted; face has been saved—and all without anguish or pangs of conscience. There is nothing to be done but to drift back off to untroubled sleep.

There can, however, be too much of a good thing. Even those with a gift for sloth must finally arrive at the point where sleeping further becomes impossible. I have known exceptionally talented alpinists who could remain unconscious for sixteen to twenty hours a day, repeatedly, but that still leaves a considerable slug of time to kill, and the less gifted, even with practice, can easily find themselves with ten or twelve waking hours to fill each day.

Boredom presents a very real, if insidious, peril. To quote Blaine Harden from the *Washington Post:* "Boredom kills, and those it does not kill, it cripples, and those it does not cripple, it bleeds like a leech, leaving its victims pale, insipid, and brooding. Examples abound . . . Rats kept in comfortable isolation quickly become jumpy, irritable, and aggressive. Their bodies twitch, their tails grow scaly." The backcountry traveler, then, in addition to developing such skills as the use of map and compass, or the prevention and treatment of blisters, must prepare mentally and materially to cope with boredom, lest his tail grow scaly.

Social creatures that we are, it is primarily to our tentmates that we turn for relief from the dullness of the socked-in camp. It is impossible to use too much care in selecting your companions. A candidate's repertoire of amusing stories, a store of gossip, and a sense of humor that blossoms under duress should be weighed at least as heavily as endurance on the trail or ice-climbing expertise.

Even more important than an ability to entertain is a personality that does not annoy. Your buddy may do a great Frank Zappa rendition, but how is that Zappa going to move you after hearing it with infrequent letup for ninety-six hours in the tent? Survivors of grim wilderness trips overwhelmingly recommend avoiding hyperactive personalities. High-strung backcountry inmates, unable to grasp the importance of procrastination and deliberation, can easily upset the delicate, sluggish ambience of the camp and exacerbate the already serious deficit of activities for filling the leaden hours.

The average mountain tent has scarcely more elbow room than a phone booth, with less floor space than a queen-size bed. When forced into such inescapable intimacy, nerves fray easily, and the pettiest irritation is quickly amplified into intolerable aggravation. Knuckle-cracking, nose-picking, snoring, and violating a tentmate's sovereign space with the soggy foot of a sleeping bag can sow the seeds of violence. During a storm-wracked trip to Mt. Deborah with his closest friend, David Roberts, one of the premier Alaskan climbers of the 1960s and 1970s, recalls:

> Our conversation either died insipidly or led to arguments. I felt so frustrated by the weather that I had to get angry at something; Don was the nearest object and the only one capable of response . . . I had got into the habit of reacting to Don's mannerisms—to the way he cleaned his knife, or held his book, or even breathed. The temptation was to invent rationalizations: I told myself that I got mad at his deliberate

△ 44

way of spooning up his breakfast cereal because it was indicative of his methodicalness, which was indicative of mental slowness, which is why he disliked and opposed my impatience . . . I was becoming, in the stagnation of our situation, both aggressive and paranoid. So I would try to keep from thinking about it; instead I would daydream about the pleasure of warmer, easier living. But all the while I would be working myself into a silent rage over the sound of Don's chewing as he ate a candy bar.

If you're worried about the psychological makeup of prospective tentmates, you might want to invest in a shelter sewn from pink fabric. Behavioral psychologists speculate that there may be hormonal neurotransmitters in the eye that are stimulated by the discrete wavelengths of certain colors. These are thought to affect the hormonal output of the brain's hypothalamus, pineal, and pituitary glands, which in turn determine mood. In a series of highly publicized experiments, test subjects were placed in a small room painted a shade known as "Baker-Miller Pink." Within fifteen minutes of entering the pink chamber, say the researchers, the subjects' muscles were tranquilized to the point of weakness, and there was a dramatic reduction in "violent, aberrant, aggressive, and self-mutilative behavior" in criminals, paranoid schizophrenics, and "obstreperous youths."

There is a good deal written about the pleasures of solitude in the great outdoors, but when you're caged in a tent, the world beyond the dank ripstop isn't doing much for you anyway. Hence the appeal of social, crowded campgrounds such as Lonesome Lake in the Wind River Range, or the Southeast Fork of the Kahiltna on Mt. McKinley. The ever-present sight and smell of trash and human waste, the thundering tape decks, and the crowds might strike the effete or uninitiated as reason to avoid them, but to those with foresight, the value of having a neighboring tent to visit when a six-day storm bears down will be obvious enough.

That it makes no sense to go into the wilderness to seek out a crowd should not be twisted into a case for heading into the wilderness in groups of one or two. By all accounts it is impossible for an extended two-person expedition to come off without inflicting permanent psychic scars on the participants if the weather turns grim. And as for going solo, Victor F. Nelson (a lifelong convict and an expert on the nuances of solitary confinement) cautioned in 1933 that "the human being, by and large, is a very bad companion for himself; where he has to face himself for any length of time, he acquires a deep disgust and a restless anxiety which makes him seek almost any escape." On a solo trip there won't be any altercations over whose turn it is to do the dishes, but when it comes right down to it, if the forecast looks bleak, most people prefer even bad company to no company at all. Quarreling at least passes the time.

Selecting a companion from one of the less temperamental species is, of course, a fine compromise between the loneliness of going solo and the likelihood of human fellowship turning rancid after a few days in a tent. A dog's conversational skills leave something to be desired, and a wet dog smells even worse than a wet climber, but a good dog will listen with tireless cheer and sympathy, and is, it goes without saying, the archetypal vent for frustration.

As the days of storm-enforced captivity mount and the dripping tent walls sag ever lower, lassitude overcomes the inmates. The eyes take on the unfocused glaze known as the "Aleutian stare," and energy for conversation becomes impossible to muster, except when it takes the form of argument. This is not a symptom peculiar to the contemporary generation of expeditionaries. In *The Worst Journey in the World*, an account of Robert Falcon Scott's doomed 1910–1913 race to the South Pole, Apsley Cherry-Garrard writes thus of weathering an antarctic winter:

> One great danger threatened all our meals in the hut, namely that of a Cag. A Cag is an argument, sometimes well informed

and always heated, upon any subject under the sun . . . They began on the smallest of excuses, they continued through the widest field to be caught up again and twisted and tortured months after . . . What caused the formation of ice crystals; . . . the best kind of crampons in the Antarctic, and the best place in London for oysters; the ideal pony rug; would the wine steward at the Ritz look surprised if you asked him for a pint of bitter?

Cherry-Garrard and company were able to resolve many of these debates by consulting the _Times Atlas_ or _Chambers Encyclopedia_. Too lazy to haul along such reliable, if heavy, reference works, present-day backcountry aficionados most often rely on the wager ("put up or shut up") to bring discussions to a close. The wise record all bets in writing.

When extemporaneous discussions become too volatile, games can provide a more structured channel for venting frustration and passing time in a civilized fashion. Botticelli is a good game, and if you bring a deck of cards, matches will substitute for poker chips, though care must be taken to keep enough of them out of tent-floor puddles to ensure hot meals. Money always seems like an exceedingly abstract commodity when you're deep in the wilds, so the game might be more exciting if stakes are limited to articles of immediate value on the trip itself—a day's rations, say if food is running short, any dry clothing that might exist, additional square inches of floor space, or meaningfully heavy portions of the load for the hike out.

Countless board games can be devised with a pen, a sleeping pad, and camp flotsam and jetsam. Recreating Monopoly is always a hit (trying to remember the correct layout of the board and the contents of the Community Chest cards can kill a lot of time in themselves), but the favorite among climbers is "Peak Experience," a long, involved game that is perversely realistic in that it can be impossible to reach the "summit." Wristwatch or hand-held electronic games are amusing, but their incessant beeping seems to have something to do with the high rate of accidental breakage while a game's owner is out visiting the latrine.

No matter how good the game, there comes a point in the latter stages of an extended incarceration when one possesses, if not out-and-out loathing, a compelling desire to minimize contact with other persons—ruling out argument or even a silent game of cards—and some type of solitary diversion becomes essential.

Though not light, books possess an ounce-of-weight to minute-of-entertainment ratio that compares quite favorably to intoxicants. One school of thought holds that life in the tent so numbs the intellect that the only literature capable of sustaining interest is simple-minded, shallow stuff, heavy on the action: science fiction, pornography, thrillers. Others recommend bringing ponderous tomes that you've always thought you should read but never quite managed: When you're sufficiently bored, after all, you'll read whatever's available, probably more than once. Indeed, why not use the unparalleled tedium of the stormed-in camp to at least get *started* on Proust?

The best tentbound reading of all, however, may be the literature of expeditioning itself, for it can be inspirational as well as enter-taining. As you sink into a morass of self-pity simply because you've spent your entire once-a-year vacation trapped inside a soggy tent that smells like dirty socks, it might help you get a grip on yourself to read about the horrors endured by such early polar explorers as Nansen, Shackelton, and Scott. Your own difficulties will be put in perspective by accounts of expeditions that lasted three years, cold that actually shattered teeth (Cherry-Garrard wrote of being thankful for a day that "warmed up" to fifty below zero), blizzards that raged at hurricane force for six weeks without letup, scurvy, starvation, and sea-leopard attack.

If interpersonal bile makes social pastimes impossible, and you've recklessly neglected to pack a book, there aren't many avenues left. Cooking and eating are of course limited by supplies of food and fuel, which are invariably meager. You can study the soup packages, memorizing the polysyllabic preservatives, or count the threads in the tent roof, but such fun cannot go on forever, and eventually you may find yourself slipping into a state described by Victor Nelson: "I would lie in bed, my face to the dark side of the cell, clinging tightly to old times and to future times . . . The contiguous, encircling reality was too harsh to be borne."

In such dire straits, even the most upstanding individuals have been known to raid the first-aid kit as a last resort. But mountain storms have a way of outlasting an emergency supply of Percodan or codeine, and a claustrophobic, smelly nylon envelope is not the best place to experience the hell of narcotic withdrawal.

Sometimes fate will smile on the tentridden, or at least smirk, and break the tedium by upping the misery level until survival itself comes into question. Getting hit by an avalanche or zapped with lightning, vaporizing the tent with an exploding stove, coming down with appendicitis two hundred miles from the nearest hospital, an attack by a grizzly—nothing cures existential ennui as quickly as an acute threat to one's existence.

There is a thin line, however, between mere wretchedness and thrilling, action-packed agony. In 1967, the first party to climb in Alaska's Revelation Mountains, finding themselves stormed in for more than forty of their fifty-two days in the range, managed to stay on the right side of that line almost continuously. Matt Hale recalls coming back to their base camp near the end of the expedition soaked to the skin after a futile, multi-day sortie to collect butterfly specimens, only to encounter a week of horizontal rain and sleet. Driven by gale-force winds right through the walls of his tent, the rain showered the interior of the shelter with a fine, continuous, thirty-four-degree spray that chilled bodies to the bone and reduced sleeping bags to sodden wads of feather and nylon.

Hale, on the verge of going hypothermic, figured out that the driest way to sleep was to remove all his wet clothing, wedge himself as best he could into his clammy but somewhat waterproof backpack (trying to ignore the fact that it was awash with the remnants of soggy Fig Newtons), pull a rain parka on over that, and only then slither into his wringing-wet sleeping bag. "Night after night," he remembers, "I'd have this delirious, half-conscious dream that I'd be hiking down the glacier and come upon a warm, dry cabin. Just as I'd start to open the door I would always wake up, shivering uncontrollably, wet and sticky with Fig Newton crumbs." Although the trials of that week in the tent covered a broad spectrum of miseries, Hale is quick to emphasize that "boredom was not a problem."

Indeed, twenty-some years after the expedition, Hale speaks of the ordeal with great affection; the guy would return to the Revelations—heinous weather and all—in an instant were the opportunity to arise. As the eminent nineteenth-century alpinist, Sir Francis Younghusband, observed, "It is because they have so much to give and give it so lavishly . . . that men love the mountains and go back to them again and again."

5. THE FLYBOYS OF TALKEETNA

IT'S AN ORDINARY JUNE MORNING IN DOWNTOWN TALKEETNA, CUL-
tural hub of Alaska's upper Susitna Valley, population maybe 250
on a good day. The dawn breeze carries the scent of spruce and
wet earth; a moose wanders across the hamlet's deserted main drag
and pauses to rub her head against the fence of the local ballpark.
Abruptly, out on the airfield at the edge of town, the peace of the
young day is shattered as the engine of a small red airplane coughs
two or three times and then catches with a roar.

The fellow in the pilot's seat is a big shaggy bear of a man named
Doug Geeting. As he taxis his craft to the end of the runway,
Geeting gets on the radio and files a flight plan in the terse, cryptic
argot that's the *lingua franca* of aviators everywhere: "Talkeetna,
four-seven-fox. We've got four souls to the Southeast Fork of the
Kahiltna. Three hours fuel. Hour-and-thirty on the route."

"Four-seven-fox, roger. Wind three-five-zero at six, favoring
three-six. Altimeter two-niner-eight-niner."

"Two-niner-eight-niner, roger. Away we go." With that, the
thirty-five-year-old pilot pulls back on the throttle, the din of the
engine rises to an unholy wail, and the little airplane leaps off the
tarmac into the huge Alaskan sky.

Beyond Talkeetna's two airstrips, half-dozen dirt streets, and
ramshackle assemblage of log cabins, trailers, quonset huts, and
souvenir shops lies a vast plain of black spruce, impenetrable alder
and waterlogged muskeg—a mosquito's idea of paradise that's flat
as a griddle and barely 350 feet above sea level. Just fifty miles
away, however, the immense ramparts of Mt. McKinley—the high-

▲ 51

est point in North America—erupt out of these lowlands without preamble. No sooner is Geeting in the air than he banks sharply to the left, buzzes west over the broad, silty braids of the Susitna River, and points the airplane squarely toward that hulking silhouette.

Geeting's craft is a Cessna 185, a six-seater with about as much room inside as a small Japanese station wagon. On this particular flight he is carrying three passengers, who are jammed into the cabin like sardines beneath a heap of backpacks, sleeping bags, skis, and mountaineering paraphernalia that fills the airplane from floor to ceiling. The three men are climbers, and they have each paid Geeting two hundred dollars to be flown to a glacier at the 7,500-foot elevation on Mt. McKinley, where they will spend the better part of a month trying to reach the 20,320-foot summit.

Approximately one thousand climbers venture onto the slopes of McKinley and its satellite peaks each year, and landing them on the high glaciers of the Alaska Range is Doug Geeting's bread and butter. "Glacier flying"—as this demanding, dangerous, little-known facet of commercial aviation is generally termed—is practiced by only a handful of pilots the world over, eight or nine of whom are based in Talkeetna. As jobs go, the pay isn't great and the hours are horrible, but the view from the office is tough to beat.

Twenty-five minutes out of Talkeetna, the first snaggle-toothed defenses of the McKinley massif rise sharply from the Susitna valley, filling the windshield of Geeting's Cessna. Ever since take-off the airplane has been laboring steadily upward. It has now reached an altitude of 8,000 feet, but the pickets of snow-plastered rock looming dead ahead stand a good 1,500 feet higher still. Geeting—who has logged some fifteen thousand hours in light planes, and has been flying this particular route for more than fifteen years now—appears supremely unconcerned as the plane bears down on the fast-approaching mountain wall.

A few moments before collision seems imminent—by which time the climbers' mouths have gone dry and their knuckles turned white—Geeting dips a wing hard, throws the plane into a dizzying right turn, and swoops through a narrow gap that appears behind the shoulder of one of the loftier spires. The walls of the mountainside flash by at such close range that individual snow crystals can be distinguished glinting in the sunlight. "Yeah," Geeting casually remarks on the other side, "that notch there was what we call 'One-Shot Pass.'

"The first rule of mountain flying," the pilot goes on to explain in the laid-back tones of his native California, "is that you never want to approach a pass straight-on, because if you get into some unexpected down draft and aren't able to clear the thing, you're going to find yourself buying the farm in a big hurry. Instead of attacking a high pass directly, I'll approach it by flying parallel to the ridge line until I'm almost alongside the pass, and then turn sharply into it so that I move through the notch at a forty-five-degree angle. That way, if I lose my lift and see that I'm not going to be high enough to make it over, I'm in position to turn away at the last instant and escape. If you want to stick around very long in this business, the idea is to leave your back door open and your stairway down and clear at all times."

On the far side of the pass is a scene straight from the Pleistocene, an alien world of black rock, blue ice, and blinding-white snow stretching from horizon to horizon. Beneath the Cessna's wings lies the Kahiltna Glacier, a tongue of ice two miles across and forty miles long, corrugated by a nubbly rash of seracs and crevasses. The scale of the setting outside the plane's windows beggars the imagination: The peaks lining the Kahiltna rise a vertical mile and more in a single sweep from glacier to summit; the avalanches that periodically rumble down these faces at a hundred-plus miles per hour have so far to travel that they appear to be falling in slow motion. Against this immense landscape, Geeting's airplane is but a miniscule red mote, an all-but-invisible mechanical gnat droning its way through the firmament toward McKinley.

Ten minutes later the gnat makes a ninety-degree turn onto a tributary of the main Kahiltna called the Southeast Fork and settles into its descent. A crude snow-landing strip, delineated by a series of plastic garbage bags tied to bamboo tomato stakes, materializes in the middle of the glacier ahead amid a maze of gargantuan crevasses. As the plane gets closer, it becomes apparent that the glacier here is far from flat, as it had appeared from a distance; the strip, in fact, lies on a slope steep enough to give a novice skier pause.

The thin air at this altitude has severely cut into the Cessna's power, and the plane will be landing uphill into a cul de sac of mile-high granite walls. Hence, Geeting cheerfully allows, "when you land here, there's no such thing as a go-around. You've got to nail your approach perfectly the first time." To avoid any unpleasant surprises, he scans the surrounding ridges for wisps of blowing snow that might tip off the existence of hazardous wind conditions. Several miles away, up at the head of the main arm of the glacier, he spies a blanket of wispy cotton-like clouds creeping over a 10,300-foot saddle called Kahiltna Pass. "Those are _foehn_ clouds," he says. "They indicate extremely turbulent downslope winds—rotors we call 'em. You can't see it, but the air is churning down those slopes like breaking surf. You take an airplane anywhere near those clouds and I guarantee you'll get the crap kicked out of you."

As if on cue, the Cessna is buffeted by a blast of severe turbulence, and the stall-warning shrieks as the airplane bucks wildly up, down, and sideways. Geeting, however, has anticipated the buffetting, and has already increased his airspeed to counter it. Serenely riding out the bumps, he guides the plane on down until the glacier rises to meet the craft's stubby aluminum skis with an easy kiss. Geeting taxis the Cessna to the uppermost end of the strip, spins the plane around with a burst of power so that it will be pointed downhill for take off, then shuts off the engine. "Well, here we are," he offers, "Kahiltna International Airport."

Geeting's passengers crawl hastily out into the glacial chill, and three other alpinists, their faces purple and peeling from a month on the hill, eagerly climb on board for a lift back to the land of beer, flush toilets, and green growing things. After five minutes at Kahiltna International, Geeting snaps off a crisp Junior Birdman salute to the dazed-looking crew he's just unloaded, fires up his Cessna one more time, and roars down the strip in a blizzard of prop-driven snow to pick up the next load of climbers, who are already impatiently awaiting his arrival back in Talkeetna.

From May through late June, the busiest climbing season on McKinley, it is not unusual for the skies over Talkeetna to reverberate with the infernal whine of ski-equipped Cessnas, Helio Couriers, and cloth-winged Super Cubs from five in the morning to well after midnight. If the racket ever cuts short anybody's beauty rest, however, no complaints are registered, for Alaska without airplanes would be as unthinkable as Iowa without corn.

"Alaskans," writes Jean Potter in *The Flying North*, a history of bush pilots, "are the flyingest people under the American flag and probably the flyingest people in the world . . . By 1939 the small airlines of the Territory were hauling twenty-three times as many passengers and a thousand times as much freight, per capita, as the airlines of the United States. The federal government and large corporations had little to do with this." The driving force behind the development of Alaskan aviation, Potter points out, was a ragtag assortment of self-reliant, seat-of-the-pants bush pilots—larger-than-life figures like Carl Ben Eielson, Joe Crosson, Noel Wien, and Bob Reeve, who cheated death on a daily basis to deliver groceries and medicine and mail to outposts at the edge of the earth—of whom Doug Geeting and his glacier-baiting rivals in Talkeetna are very much the spiritual heirs.

A 12,800-foot peak overlooking Kahiltna International's makeshift glacial airstrip now bears the name of Joe Crosson, which is fitting, because it was Crosson, in April, 1932, who pulled off the first Alaskan glacier landing, on McKinley's Muldrow Glacier, where he delivered a scientific expedition to measure cosmic rays. According to one of the expedition members, Crosson took the momentous initial landing "much as a matter of course, and lit a cigar before leaving the plane," though Jean Potter reports that the job resulted in "such risk and such damage" to the aircraft that Crosson's employer, Alaskan Airways, subsequently forbade him to engage in any further glacier sorties.

It was left to Bob Reeve—a high-strung Wisconsin-born barnstormer and bon vivant—to perfect the art of glacier flying. Beginning in 1929, the twenty-seven-year-old Reeve had been introduced to mountain aviation while pioneering extremely hazardous long-distance air-mail routes over the Andes of South America between Lima, Santiago, and Buenos Aires, where he occasionally shared a bottle between flights with a dapper, romantic French airman named Antoine de Saint-Exupéry, who would soon thereafter write both *The Little Prince* and an intensely lyrical, hugely popular record of the early flying life, *Wind, Sand, and Stars*.

Reeve left South America in 1932 after incurring the wrath of his superiors by smashing up an expensive Lockheed Vega. Back in the States, he promptly lost all his money in the stock market and contracted polio. Finding himself flat broke and seriously ill at the height of the depression, he stowed away on a freighter to Alaska seeking a change of luck, and wound up in the seedy port city of Valdez.

Unfortunately, Alaska had already attracted a host of hungry pilots in those depression years, and there weren't enough paying customers to go around. Desperate for work, Reeve decided to specialize in a corner of the aviation market that not even the territory's boldest aviators had dared to go after: landing gold miners and their heavy supplies on the glaciers that flowed down from the jumble of high peaks surrounding Valdez. By trial and error, Reeve quickly developed a sense for steering clear of hidden crevasses, discovered that the incline of a glacier could be an aid, rather than an impediment, to making short-field landings and take offs, and learned that by dropping a line of spruce boughs or gunny sacks onto the snow before setting down, he could establish a horizon and judge the lay of a slope on cloudy days when it was otherwise impossible to tell exactly where the ground was.

Reeve also figured out how to keep his glacier-flying business solvent in the spring and summer months, when there was still enough snow to land high in the mountains, but not enough to enable a ski-equipped plane to take off from the sea-level airfield in Valdez: He sheathed the bottoms of the plane's wooden skis with stainless steel he'd scrounged from an abandoned cocktail bar, and, for a summer runway, took to using the mud flats of Valdez Bay, which turned into a slippery plain of silt and eel grass between tides.

When Bradford Washburn—a high-powered mountaineer and geographer who would later become director of Boston's Museum of Science—heard that Reeve was in the business of making year-round glacier landings, he immediately wrote to the pilot to inquire if he'd be willing to land a climbing expedition on a remote glacier beneath 17,150-foot Mt. Lucania, which was the highest unclimbed mountain in North America at the time. It was a dicey proposition, entailing 480 miles of flying over rough, uncharted country, and landing at an altitude two thousand feet higher than had ever been accomplished in a heavily loaded ski plane. Nevertheless, says Washburn, "Ten days after I'd sent the letter, I got back a telegram that said, in its entirety, 'Anywhere you'll ride, I'll fly. Bob Reeve.'"

The first flight to Lucania to cache six hundred pounds of supplies, in early May, 1937, went off without a hitch, but when Reeve returned a month later to deliver Washburn and another climber named Bob Bates, the Fairchild 51 sank to its belly in wet, bottomless snow as soon as it touched down: unusually warm temperatures had turned the glacier into a sea of slush. The three men managed to dig the plane out and pull it to firmer ground, but Reeve became hopelessly mired again every time he tried to take off, wasting so much fuel in the process that it was doubtful whether enough remained for the flight back to Valdez.

△ 57

He was marooned for four days and nights. On the fifth morning, as it was beginning to look like the plane was destined to become a permanent fixture on the glacier, slightly cooler temperatures formed a thin crust over the slush. Reeve tossed out all his tools and emergency equipment to lighten the aircraft, flattened the pitch of the propellor with a wrench to squeeze every last bit of horsepower out of the engine, and then committed the plane down the slope toward the lip of an ice cliff.

"He dropped out of sight over the crest of the glacier," Washburn remembers, "and there was silence. Bates and I were sure he'd crashed. Then, suddenly, we heard the roar of the engine and the plane climbed back into sight. Reeve had made it into the air by the skin of his teeth." By the time the Fairchild splashed down on the Valdez mud flats, the plane was sputtering along on the last vapors in the fuel tanks.

Washburn came away from the Lucania trip deeply impressed with Reeve, and went on to hire him for several subsequent expeditions. By the 1950s, though, Reeve had moved on from Valdez and was unavailable for glacier work, so Washburn was forced to turn elsewhere when he needed a full-time pilot for an ongoing nine-year cartographic survey of Mt. McKinley. A fearless young Talkeetna-based flyer named Don Sheldon was recommended. Washburn says that when he asked Reeve what he knew about Sheldon, Reeve replied, "He's either crazy and he's going to kill himself, or he'll turn out to be one hell of a good pilot." The latter proved to be the case.

Taking advantage of the newly invented "wheel-ski" landing gear—which permitted a pilot to take off with wheels on a dry runway, and then, while airborne, lower a set of skis into position for landing on snow—Sheldon flew commercially out of Talkeetna for twenty-seven years, routinely logging more than eight hundred hours each summer in the malevolent skies over the Alaska Range. Along the way he went through forty-five airplanes—four of them totaled in violent crashes—but he never injured either himself or a single passenger. His nervy high-altitude landings and life-saving rescue missions were legendary not only throughout Alaska, but in much of the world at large. At the time of his death from colon cancer in 1975, the name Don Sheldon had become synonymous with heroic glacier flying.

Sheldon's career coincided with the mushrooming popularity of mountaineering on McKinley; over the last decade of his life Sheldon was so busy flying climbers that in the spring and summer months he averaged just four or five hours of sleep a night. Even with the onerous workload, though, most years Sheldon barely made enough money to pay the bills. "Nobody gets rich owning an air-taxi business," explains Roberta Reeve Sheldon—Don's widow and Bob Reeve's daughter—who still lives in Talkeetna in a modest wood-frame house at the end of the village airstrip. "All the money you make goes back into the airplanes. I remember once we went to the bank and borrowed forty thousand dollars to buy a new Cessna 180. Three months later Don totaled it on Mt. Hayes. I'll tell you, it hurts to be making payments on an airplane you don't even have anymore."

Sheldon's financial woes were exacerbated by the existence of a second, equally talented glacier pilot in town, one Cliff Hudson, who started working out of Talkeetna a few years after Sheldon did. It was not a friendly rivalry: Sheldon and Hudson were forever stealing each other's customers, and longtime Talkeetnans still vividly recall a fistfight between the two pilots that splintered the candy counter in the B & K Trading Post and left both men with black eyes and split lips. Things got so bad between them that Sheldon once allegedly buzzed Hudson at extremely close range in midair, an incident that wound up in the courts and nearly cost Sheldon his license.

Sheldon—a cocky, ruggedly handsome ex-cowboy from Wyoming—looked every inch the dashing bush pilot. In marked contrast, Hudson—who is still alive and flying—might easily be mistaken for a stray panhandler from the Bowery, thanks to the soiled wool shirt, shiny polyester slacks, and cheesy black loafers that make up his standard flight uniform. Hudson's sartorial shortcomings, however, haven't diminished his reputation as a masterful glacier pilot.

The primary wind sock for the village airstrip sits atop the roof of an infamous local watering hole called the Fairview Inn. It is not uncommon, within the Fairview's dimly lit chambers, to overhear barstool aviators bickering over the relative abilities of Hudson and Sheldon in the manner of baseball fans comparing Maris and Ruth. There are denizens of the Fairview who argue that Hudson is at least as good a pilot as Sheldon was, pointing out that Hudson—incredibly—has yet to wreck a single airplane despite having logged more hours of glacier flying than any other man alive.

After Sheldon's death, Hudson enjoyed a few relatively flush years without serious competition, but only a few: by 1984 there were no fewer than four air-taxi companies operating full-time out of Talkeetna—Hudson Air Service, Doug Geeting Aviation, K2 Aviation, and Talkeetna Air Taxi—all specializing in glacier flying, and all headed by brilliant pilots hell-bent on being top dog. Jim Okonek, the owner of K2 Aviation, candidly allows that "each of us considers himself the best pilot in town, and can't imagine why a person would ever want to fly with anybody else."

Not surprisingly, the confluence of so many robust egos in such a small place throws off sparks from time to time. Insults are traded, clients are rustled. The pilots are constantly reporting each other to the authorities for real or imagined breaches of regulations. The friction has lately escalated to the point where Geeting will no longer speak to either Okonek or Lowell Thomas, Jr., the owner of Talkeetna Air Taxi. The bad blood between Geeting and Thomas runs so thick that Thomas—a gentlemanly sixty-four-year-old ex-lieutenant governor of Alaska and son of the famous broadcaster—can't even bear to utter Geeting's name: When a conversation requires that Thomas acknowledge the existence of his younger rival, Thomas simply refers to Geeting as "that other fellow."

The only time the pilots put their differences aside is when they participate in the annual Memorial Day Fly-over, during which airplanes from each of the four companies buzz low over the Talkeetna cemetery in tight formation, wingtip-to-wingtip, in a tribute to Talkeetna's war dead. It's a stirring sight. Not even for this momentous event, however, will Geeting and Okonek deign to speak to each other.

The competition in Talkeetna these days has motivated the pilots to seek out a clientele beyond the traditional fare of mountaineers, surveyors, hunters, and miners. Geeting, for example, has contracted with the Department of Fish and Game to fly misbehaving grizzly bears to distant corners of the Alaska Range. During one such flight, the unrestrained passenger awoke from a drugged stupor and expressed her displeasure by shredding the plane's upholstery before Geeting managed to land and push her out the door.

Of the four air-taxi owners, Okonek has been the most enterprising at drumming up new business. Not long ago he flew a photographer and a bevy of young women to the Great Gorge of the Ruth Glacier, one of the most spectacular stretches of the McKinley massif, whereupon the ladies immediately stripped to the buff and posed on the ice for what would become a memorable *Playboy* magazine feature titled "The Women of Alaska." "If you hope to make it in this business, you have to be resourceful," Okonek offers. "With so many pilots in town, there just aren't enough climbers to go around."

In addition to bears and bunnies, all of the pilots now regularly take planeloads of tourists, ordinary vacationers from Philadelphia and Des Moines, on sight-seeing flights to the glaciers. These trips have become so routine, in fact, that cynics suggest that the risk and romance has all but disappeared from the job—that glacier flying today isn't much different from driving a cab. Okonek, a retired Air Force colonel who flew helicopters in Viet Nam, disagrees, insisting that "this has got to be the best flying job anywhere. Jacques Cousteau's pilot recently called to ask me for a job; top commercial pilots from all over the world have expressed interest in working here.

"I take quite a few airline pilots up to the glacier on their layover days," Okonek continues, "guys who fly 747s for Swissair and Qantas, and it bowls them over to see the places we land, the terrain we fly over. Glacier flying still holds plenty of challenge. Pilots lacking mountain experience will fly up the Kahiltna for a look around and get disoriented by the incredible scale of the peaks. All of a sudden their little airplane is out of breath, they're out of ideas about what to do, and they crash onto the glacier. We see it year after year."

And green, amateur flyers are not the only ones who smash airplanes into the Alaska Range. In 1981, an experienced Talkeetna pilot named Ed Homer took two friends on an afternoon joyride around McKinley, got caught in a downdraft while crossing Kahiltna Pass, and slammed his Cessna into the mountainside. By the time rescuers reached the wreckage four days later, one passenger was dead, the other had lost both his hands to frostbite and Homer had lost both his feet. "We're often up against a fine line in this business," Lowell Thomas emphasizes. "It's just a question of whether you can recognize when you're stepping too far over that line. And there are definitely times—usually when we're called upon to rescue climbers who've gotten themselves into trouble—when we step over the line quite a ways, and do things that are extremely marginal."

Geeting handles more than his share of those marginal flights. Several years ago, a climber plunged seventy feet into a hidden crevasse on Mt. Foraker—a 17,400-foot peak next to McKinley—and suffered massive head injuries. After two days of stormy weather stymied several rescue attempts, a doctor on the scene radioed in desperation that the victim would die if he didn't get to a hospital soon. "It was completely socked-in," Geeting recalls. "Visibility was zero-zero from the surface of the glacier all the way up to eleven thousand feet. But I'd landed beneath Foraker before, and I'd memorized the layout of the surrounding peaks and ridges, so I decided to take a shot at evacuating the guy."

Geeting's plan was to approach Foraker above the clouds, get his bearings, and then establish a precise descent pattern into the soup. "I'd fly straight for exactly one minute," he explains, "then turn for one minute, fly straight for another minute, turn again for a minute. It was a total whiteout—I couldn't see a freaking thing—but I trusted the course I'd worked out ahead of time and stuck to it. For a reference point, I asked the people on the glacier to give me a shout on the radio every time they heard me pass overhead."

From the time he dropped into the cloud bank, Geeting was irrevocably committed. The peaks looming unseen in the mists beyond his wingtips left absolutely no room for error: If the pilot were to complete a turn a few seconds late, or steer a few degrees too far to the left or right, with each subsequent maneuver he would unwittingly compound the mistake, and the airplane would eventually plow blindly into one of a dozen icy mountainsides at 110 miles per hour.

"I made my way down through the cloud between the mountain walls," Geeting says, "watching the compass, the clock, and the altimeter real close, listening for the climbers to yell, 'Now!' when I buzzed over them. I figured touchdown would be right at seven thousand feet, so when the altimeter showed seventy-five hundred I lined up for final, slowed to landing speed and went on in. It was a real odd feeling, because in a whiteout like that you can't tell where the sky stops and the glacier begins. All of a sudden my airspeed went down to nothing, and I thought, 'Son of a bitch!' Then I looked out the window and saw these climbers running out of the cloud toward the airplane. Damned if I wasn't on the ground."

△ 63

6. CLUB DENALI

BEFORE THEY'LL LET YOU CLIMB MT. MCKINLEY, THE RANGERS WHO oversee mountaineering in Denali National Park make you sit through a tape and slide presentation depicting the perils of venturing onto the highest mountain in North America, in much the same way that the army, before granting off-base passes to new recruits, shows them films depicting the ravages of venereal disease. The ten-minute Denali show runs heavily to images of thundering avalanches, storm-flattened tents, hands deformed by horrible frostbite blisters, and grotesquely twisted bodies being pulled from the depths of enormous crevasses. Like the military's VD movies, the Denali show is graphic enough to make even the thickest skin crawl. As a tool for promoting sensible behavior, it would appear that it's also just as ineffective.

Take, for example, the case of Adrian Popovich, better known as Adrian the Romanian. A few years ago Adrian—a loud man in his midtwenties, possessing darkly handsome features and a volatile temper—somehow managed to flee his homeland, one of the Eastern Bloc's more cheerless satellites, and find his way to the western United States. He had done some climbing in Romania, enough to realize that he had a natural gift for it, and upon his arrival in America decided to pursue the sport seriously. Toward that end he spent most of his days hanging out at the "Rock" in Seattle—a thirty-foot concrete escarpment on the University of Washington campus where swarms of steel-fingered, Lycra-clad young men and women hone their 5.13 moves and engage in spirited bouldering duels.

▲ 64

Adrian developed into one of the hotter climbers at the Rock, and it fanned the flames of his ambition: He announced his intention to solo McKinley in the spring of 1986, and thereby become the first Romanian to stand atop the highest peak in North America. Upon hearing this, cynics were quick to point out that the challenges of McKinley were somewhat different from those posed by even the gnarliest routes on the Rock. They further noted that it was impossible, in the strict sense of the word, to "solo" a climb while in close proximity to some three hundred people, that being the number of other climbers Adrian could expect to encounter on the route he intended to try. Adrian, however, was not about to be dissuaded by such niggling.

Nor, upon arriving in Alaska, was he to be dissuaded when, in the course of registering for his climb, a mild-mannered ranger named Ralph Moore suggested that it was suicidal to attempt McKinley without a tent, or a shovel to dig snow caves, or a stove, all of which Adrian lacked. Without the latter to melt snow, Moore queried, just what did Adrian intend to drink during the three weeks it typically takes to climb the mountain? "I have money," Adrian replied as if nothing could be more obvious, "I will buy water from other climbers."

Adrian was shown the grisly slide presentation; he was apprised of the fact that McKinley had killed more climbers than the Eiger; it was explained to him that by the time he was only halfway up the 20,320-foot peak he could expect to find conditions more severe than those at the North Pole, with temperatures of forty below zero and winds that howled at 80 to 100 miles per hour for days and sometimes weeks at a stretch; he was given a booklet that cautioned, among other things, that on McKinley "the combined effect of cold, wind, and altitude may well present one of the most hostile climates on Earth." Adrian's reaction to these caveats was to propose angrily that the rangers mind their own business.

Moore, who had no authority to keep Adrian off the mountain (and whose responsibility it would be to rescue Adrian or retrieve his body should either be called for), ultimately resigned himself to the fact that nothing was going to persuade the hotheaded Romanian to abandon his plans. All the ranger could do was try to see that somebody loaned Adrian a stove and a tent, and hope luck turned out to be on the guy's side.

It did, at least in the sense that Adrian didn't die. He actually managed to make it all the way to 19,000 feet without falling into any hidden crevasses or getting frostbite. But he had been too impatient in his ascent to acclimatize thoroughly, and he let himself become seriously dehydrated as well, thus violating two of the most fundamental rules of self-preservation at high altitude. As he plodded alone up the penultimate slopes, gasping at the thin, frigid air, he began to feel increasingly nauseous and dizzy, and began to stumble like a drunk.

Adrian was experiencing the onset of cerebral edema, a deadly swelling of the brain brought on by ascending too high, too fast. Terrified by what was happening to him, finding it harder and harder to think clearly or stand up, he nonetheless succeeded in dragging himself back down to 14,300 feet, whence he and another would-be soloist—a Japanese whose feet were so badly frostbitten that all ten toes had to be amputated—were evacuated by glacier pilot Lowell Thomas to a hospital in Anchorage. When Adrian was handed a bill for his share of this risky air rescue, he refused to pay, leaving the National Park Service to pick up the tab.

The mountain that officially bears the surname of our twenty-fifth president (an appellation that is largely and pointedly ignored by climbers in favor of "Denali," the peak's Athabascan name) is so big that it beggars the imagination: One of the largest landforms on the planet, McKinley's hulking massif occupies 120 square miles of the earth's surface, and its summit stands more than 17,000 vertical feet above the rolling tundra at the mountain's foot. Mt. Everest, by comparison, rises a mere 12,000 feet from the plains at its base.

McKinley's bitterly contested summit was first reached in 1913 from the north by a party led by Hudson Stuck, the Episcopal archdeacon of the Yukon. It took nineteen years for the peak to be climbed again, but in the ensuing decades approximately five thousand people have joined the Reverend Stuck. Along the way, McKinley has seen some memorable feats and personalities.

In 1961 the great Italian alpinist, Ricardo Cassin, led a team up the elegant granite buttress that bisects the mountain's south face, an impressive enough achievement to prompt a congratulatory cable from President John Kennedy. In 1963 seven brash Harvard students took a route directly up the center of the 14,000 foot, avalanche-swept Wickersham Wall, an act so bold or foolish that, twenty-four years later, it still hasn't been repeated. In the 1970s and 1980s such bona fide heroes as Reinhold Messner, Doug Scott, Dougal Haston, and Renato Casarotto visited McKinley and left challenging new lines in their wakes.

Most people who attempt McKinley, it is safe to assume, do not do so seeking the solitude of the great outdoors. There are currently more than twenty different routes to the summit, but an overwhelming majority of those who attempt the mountain do so by a single line, the West Buttress, a route pioneered by Bradford Washburn in 1951. In 1987, in fact, nearly 700 of the 817 climbers on McKinley thronged to the "Butt," as it is affectionately known. During the peak climbing months of May and June, while nearby faces and ridges are often completely empty, lines of climbers cover the West Buttress like ants. So many people try the route, Jonathan Waterman writes in _Surviving Denali_, that at the higher elevations where gale-force winds regularly scour all fresh snow from the slopes soon after it falls, climbers must "select cooking snow very carefully from among the wasteland of brown turds . . . Fortunately, sometimes below 15,000 feet, snowfall will cover the excrement, the bodies, the trash, and the jettisoned gear."

The typical McKinley climber drops, on average, between $2,000 and $3,500 (a sum that rises to $3,500 to $5,000 if he climbs with

△ 67

a commercial guide service, as forty percent of McKinley climbers do), and subjects himself to three weeks of exceedingly cruel and unusual punishment. He does so not in order to commune with nature, but because he (or she: perhaps ten percent of McKinley climbers are women) wants very badly to add the pinnacle of North America to his trophy collection. And by ganging up on the West Buttress—the easiest way up the mountain—he hopes to stack the odds in his favor as much as possible. Most years, McKinley still wins about half the time. Some years it does even better. In April and May of 1987, for instance, Park Service records show that six out of every seven climbers on the mountain went home in defeat. One of them was me.

Things began well enough. When I arrived in Talkeetna, the time-honored point of embarkation for McKinley expeditions, I expected to have to wait the customary three or four days for flying weather, as I had the last time I'd flown into the Alaska Range, twelve years before. I was thus pleasantly surprised, just fourteen hours after pulling into town, to find myself shoehorned into the back of a small red Cessna owned by ace pilot Doug Geeting. Forty minutes later I was delivered intact to Kahiltna International Airport: a rutted snow landing strip on the lower Kahiltna Glacier. Exactly 13,320 vertical feet above the airstrip, and fifteen circuitous miles to the north, the summit of McKinley glistened in a flawless sky.

To be torn from the security of Talkeetna's Fairview Inn and dropped into a landscape of vertical granite and avalanching ice that dwarfed the human form to utter insignificance was rather disquieting, but every fifteen minutes another Cessna or Helio-courier would buzz out of the sky to disgorge a load of climbers, and the swelling ranks beside the landing strip went a long way toward softening the shock of the inhospitable new surroundings.

Thirty or forty tents were dug into the slope above Kahiltna International's crude runway, housing an army of climbers who were hooting and yelling at one another in at least five languages as they inventoried supplies and packed their loads for the climb ahead. Rob Stapleton—a tall, dour man hired jointly by the various competing glacier pilots to live at Kahiltna International and try to maintain some semblance of order—shook his head at it all and speculated that some of the folks around him were headed for trouble. "It's amazing," he opined, "how unorganized and fucked-up a lot of the groups already are by the time they get here. Too many of these guys are operating on about ninety percent energy and ten percent brains."

This collective energy, misplaced or not, was a welcome antidote to the unrelieved drudgery of the slog from the airstrip up the lower glaciers, a 7,000-foot elevation gain that most parties take a week to cover. I had come to Alaska alone, but as I skied up the Kahiltna each day I would inevitably be absorbed by one or another genial, funky procession—a seemingly endless line of climbers, trudging stoically upward with teetering, hundred-pound loads that brought to mind scenes of the Klondike gold rush. For that first week the weather was all anyone could ask for: At night the air had a wintry bite, and enough snow fell to make for some memorable after-dinner powder skiing, but the days were generally filled with sun.

Occasionally a knot of climbers, already having met defeat, would pass in descent, offering warnings of sledgehammer winds and hellish cold above 14,000 feet, but those of us on our way up maintained a smug conviction that conditions would be different by the time we got up high. Even after encountering two Scotsmen whose teammate had just been helicoptered off the mountain with severe brain damage after taking an eight-hundred-foot tumble, and two other climbers on their way down after nearly dying from pulmonary edema—first a Yugoslav, then a Pole, both with Him-alayan experience—the optimism of those fresh off the Cessnas remained unshakable.

When registering climbers for McKinley, the rangers ask that each party provide them, for record-keeping purposes, with an official expedition name. The expeditions with whom I shared the mountain chose such official designations as "The Walking Heads," "Fat Rod," and "Dick Danger and the Throbbing Members." Upon pulling into the large camp at 14,300 feet that climbers use as a launching pad for assaults on the upper peak, I threw my pack down near a couple of Throbbing Members, who were in a heated argument with another climber.

"I tell you something, big guy," the non-Member spat contemptuously, "in my country you do that, they line you up and shoot you!" I had no idea what the discussion was about, but there was no mistaking that heavily accented voice, which I'd heard ranting similarly on many occasions at the Rock in Seattle: Adrian the Romanian was back on McKinley. You had to admire the guy's nerve, I thought: The rangers were still fuming about being stiffed for his last rescue bill.

Adrian, however, had had plenty of time to mull over the debacle of the year before, and was determined not to fail again. "All winter, it is all I can think about," he explained. "It make me crazy." Though he had again come alone, this year he'd assembled a full arsenal of top-of-the-line gear, including not one but *two* tents, and had double-carried enough food and fuel to 14,300 feet to stay on the upper mountain for two full months if need be, an approach that reflected a more enlightened view of acclimatization.

He had, in fact, already been up to 19,000 feet on two occasions, and had prudently turned around both times because conditions were less than perfect. "I tell you something," the new Adrian was now in the habit of admonishing anyone he could buttonhole, "this is very big mountain. You make one little mistake, it really kick your ass." From the looks of the way the camp was dug in, by the time most people had reached 14,300 feet they were starting to believe it.

The "camp" was in reality a full-blown tent city, with a population that fluctuated between 40 and 120 as parties came and went. It spread across the edge of a desolate glacial plateau. To one side, the upper ramparts of the mountain soared in a single sweep of granite and snow and gleaming blue ice, culminating in the summit more than a vertical mile above; to the other side, the flat shelf of the plateau ran for several hundred yards before breaking off abruptly in a clean four-thousand-foot drop.

To prevent their tents from being ripped from their moorings and blown off that drop, climbers had taken to placing their shelters in deep bunkers surrounded by massive snow-block walls. The walls lent the camp a battlefield air, as if a barrage of incoming artillery might be expected at any moment. Carving such bunkers is a formidable chore, so when I found a good, deep one that had recently been vacated I immediately laid claim to it, even though it was located in one of the seedier neighborhoods, next to the camp's continually busy communal latrine: a plywood throne, completely open to the elements, that had an inspiring view but left tender flesh dangerously exposed to the full brunt of a windchill that regularly dipped below minus-seventy degrees.

The opposite side of camp, the high-rent district, was distinguished by a complex of igloos, bombproof dome tents, and propane-heated Weatherports that served as the offices and residences of Dr. Peter H. Hackett and his staff. Every summer since 1982, Hackett—a lean, laconic, tired-looking climber/physician who is the world's foremost authority on high-altitude pathology—has set up shop at 14,300 feet to conduct research into the mysterious ailments that afflict humans at altitude. He comes here, he said, because he can always count on finding a reliable supply of very sick climbers to study: "Lots of people on McKinley don't know what they're getting into, and climb too fast, and become seriously ill. Fresh guinea pigs are always staggering in the door." At least a dozen of these guinea pigs would now be dead were it not for the ministrations of Hackett's team.

Hackett was quick to emphasize that "we never perform experiments on walk-in patients that we wouldn't perform on ourselves." At that very moment, for example, his research partner, Rob Roach,

△ 71

was in the process of testing a new, blue-colored medication for altitude illness on himself. From the green cast of Roach's skin, and the blue vomit splattered over his white vapor-barrier boots, it appeared that the new drug was less than completely effective.

Hackett's team, I later learned, not only received no remuneration for their lifesaving labors, but—having failed to obtain funding in both 1986 and 1987—met most of the project's expenses out of their own pockets. I asked one of the doctors, Howard Donner, why they volunteered to spend their summers toiling in such a godforsaken place. "Well," he explained as he stood shivering in a blizzard, reeling from nausea and a blinding headache while attempting to repair a broken radio antenna, "it's sort of like having fun, only different."

The West Buttress of McKinley, it is often said, has all the technical challenges of a long walk in the snow. That is more or less true, but it's also true that if you should, say, trip on a bootlace at the wrong moment during that walk, you will probably die. From 16,000 feet to 17,000 feet, for instance, the route follows the crest of a knife-edge ridge that presents a two-thousand-foot drop on one side and a three-thousand-foot drop on the other. Furthermore, even the flattest, most benign-looking terrain can be riddled with hidden crevasses, many of which are big enough to swallow a Greyhound bus, no problem.

Not that a crevasse has to be huge to be dangerous. In February, 1984, Naomi Uemura—the renowned Japanese mountaineer and polar explorer—disappeared in mid-descent after completing the first solo winter ascent of McKinley. It is widely believed that he met his end in one of the relatively small crevasses that split the broad slope between the camp at 14,300 feet and the knife-edge ridge at 16,000. Indeed, last spring a pair of newlyweds from Denver almost ended their honeymoon (for reasons known only to them, they had decided to spend it on McKinley) in one of those same slots.

△ 72

The Honeymooners—the name under which the expedition of Ellie and Conrad Miller was officially registered—were camped with Adrian the Romanian and three other expeditions in a crowded, poorly protected tenement of a bunker that happened to be next door to mine at 14,300 feet. On May 16 the Millers climbed to 17,200 feet to cache a load of food and fuel for a later summit push. That evening they were descending back to their camp at 14,300 when Conrad, who was in the lead, suddenly broke through a thin snow bridge and found himself plummeting through space, "ricocheting like a pinball" between the walls of a narrow but very deep crevasse.

The slope above this crevasse was fairly steep, and the force of Conrad's fall jerked Ellie off her feet and pulled her down toward the hole through which he'd dropped. A split second before Ellie, too, would have disappeared into the crevasse, she managed to sink the pick of her ice axe and bring them both to a stop.

Dangling fifty feet below the surface in the blue twilight of the crevasse, Conrad first made a quick examination of his trousers to see if his sphincter had let go (it hadn't), then checked for broken bones (there were none). Then, with Ellie tugging on the rope from above, he slowly front-pointed up one of the vertical walls of the slot. As he struggled back to the surface, Conrad was gripped with the conviction that had he gone all the way to the bottom, still hundreds of feet below, "The last thing I would have seen would have been Uemura's frozen corpse."

Both Conrad, a thirty-six-year-old architect, and Ellie, a 28-year-old retail clerk, were badly shaken, but they were also very determined to get to the summit of McKinley. On May 18—despite the fact that it had been storming for days and an even bigger storm was in the forecast—they headed back up to 17,200 feet, intending to recover their cache, hang tough until the weather got better, and then make a dash for the top.

But the storm, which grew worse that day, proved to be considerably more severe and of considerably longer duration than the

Honeymooners had reckoned. Temperatures at 17,200 feet dropped to minus-fifty, and gale-force winds raked the peak almost without letup for more than a week, driving the wind chill well down into triple digits. Not only was climbing out of the question, so was sleeping; Conrad and Ellie were reduced for the most part to lying in their tent with all their extra clothes on, praying that their shelter didn't blow apart at the seams. (Indeed, shortly before the Honeymooners arrived at 17,200, an Oval Intention—one of the sturdiest tents made—had done just that, exploding in the middle of the night, leaving its three occupants in a very bad way.)

The gale that blasted the upper peak during this storm was terrifying to behold, even from the relative safety of 14,300 feet. Whenever the wind lulled at the lower camp, a much deeper, wilder, wailing roar—like the thunder of a rocket launch—could be heard emanating from the ridge three thousand feet above. At the onset of the storm, most of the twenty or thirty climbers who had been camped at 17,200 immediately bailed out and battled their way back down to 14,300, but not the Honeymooners.

Early in their stay at 17,200, Conrad and Ellie spied the entrance to an ice cave. Thinking it had to offer more secure accommodations than their tent, Ellie went over to investigate. It turned out to be a T-shaped affair, carved deep into the slope, with a fifteen-foot-long entrance tunnel that led to a perpendicular main tunnel at least twice that length. It was, without question, infinitely more storm-proof than the tent, but the briefest tour of the premises convinced Ellie that she'd rather take her chances out in the maelstrom.

The inside of that cave, she says, "was incredibly grim: really dark and damp, and extremely claustrophobic. The place was a hellhole; it was absolutely hideous. There was no way I was going to move into that thing."

The tunnels were only four feet high, garbage littered the floor, the walls were stained with urine and vomit and God only knew what else. Most disturbing of all, though, were the creatures she found inhabiting that subterranean gloom. "There were seven or eight very strange guys in there," Ellie says. "They'd been in the cave for days, and had long since run out of food. They were just sitting there, shivering with all their extra clothes on in the suffocating air; breathing these thick stove fumes and singing theme songs from TV shows, getting stranger and stranger. I couldn't get out of there fast enough."

The cave men, as it happened, were members of two separate expeditions. One of them—a trio from Flagstaff, Arizona, who called themselves the Crack o'Noon Club—had actually only been in there a day or so. The other, decidedly stranger, group had been in the cave for the better part of a week. It turned out to be none other than Dick Danger and the Throbbing Members.

Dick and the Members—a.k.a. Michael Dagon, Greg Siewers, Jeff Yates, and Stephen "Este" Parker—were four tough, arrogant, in-your-face Alaskans in their late twenties and early thirties. They possessed very little in the way of mountaineering experience, but they had done their homework and were bent on bagging the summit of McKinley at almost any cost. Dagon—Dick Danger himself—had sworn off red meat and alcohol for a year to prepare for the expedition, and had trained and schemed so obsessively that his wife had left him.

The Members, it seems, had arrived at 14,300 on May 9; a day later, Yates came down with pulmonary edema—a mild case, but a gurgling, wheezing, potentially life-threatening case of edema nonetheless. Most climbers would have promptly retreated, but the three healthy Members left Yates to recover for a day at 14,300, carried a cache of food up to 16,000 feet, and then returned to 14,300 for the night. The next morning, having decided that Yates wasn't getting any worse, all four of them headed up onto the knife-edge ridge to establish a high camp in preparation for a summit bid.

When the Members arrived at 17,200 feet on May 13, they took up residence in their tents in a poorly built bunker alongside the sturdier bunkers of a half-dozen other expeditions, including a party of Park Service personnel led by ranger Scott Gill, a group led by a seasoned Alaskan guide named Brian Okonek, and a vacationing SWAT team from the Montreal police force. At the time, the Members figured they had enough food for three days, maybe four if they stretched it. By the eighteenth it was still storming, and the food was almost gone.

To complicate matters, that afternoon ranger Gill received a weather report over the radio predicting that an even nastier storm front—the forecasters were calling it "a major three-day storm"—was due to slam into the upper mountain within a matter of hours. When a voice cut in over the radio to ask just how major, the person relaying the forecast replied with a macabre chuckle, "Well, major enough so that when it hits, everyone who's above 15,000 feet is going to die."

"All of a sudden," Yates says, "it was like, 'Wow, maybe we'd better be getting out of here.' " He reports that other teams "started booking down from 17,200 right away, but it took us three hours to pack up, and by the time we'd gotten underway the storm was on us for real. Right away we lost the trail in the whiteout. The wind was so bad that someone in the last party to leave camp ahead of us had to abandon his pack to keep going. By the time we were two rope-lengths away it was obvious we weren't going to make it, so we turned around and headed back up to 17,200."

At that point, says Dagon, "We figured we were in deep shit." They re-erected their tents and anchored them to the slope with snow pickets and an elaborate web of climbing rope, but feared that the rising gale would still rip the shelters right off the ridge. It was at that point that Brian Okonek, secure enough in his heavy bunker, told them about the ice cave. He had built it, he said, during a bad storm in 1983, and it saved the lives of eighteen climbers.

The intervening years had plugged Okonek's cave full of drifting snow, and it took the Members, assisted by another expedition called 5150, six hours of cold, hard digging—during which all four Members received frostbitten fingers and toes—to re-excavate it. Once they were all moved in, however, they took a perverse liking to cave life: Despite frostbite and lack of food, they resolved to wait out the storm, no matter how long it took, and go bag the summit.

Life at 14,300 feet, meanwhile, was undeniably better than the wretched existence of those dug in at 17,200, but it was not without its hardships. Trapped in camp but relatively free of the storm that raged above, we residents of 14,300 initially bided our time cheerfully enough—flying kites, skiing the crusty powder on the protected slopes immediately above camp, practicing ice climbing on nearby serac walls. But as the storm dragged on—and food, fuel, and energy began to flag—a collective depression settled over our embattled tent city.

When word came over the radio in the medical tent confirming rumors that five well-liked climbers had been killed in avalanches on the neighboring peaks of Mt. Foraker and Mt. Hunter, the air of gloom deepened further still. People took to staying in their miserable little bunkers day-in and day-out, bickering and shivering inside their tents, emerging only to visit the latrine or shovel out from under the snowdrifts. "It was your idea to come on this fucking expedition," I overheard a climber in a nearby tent whining to his partner, "I told you we should have gone rock climbing in Yosemite!"

As the storm continued, trade in critical supplies became brisk and cutthroat. Expeditions with an abundance of some particularly valuable commodity like toilet paper, cigarettes, Diamox (a medication to prevent altitude sickness), or Tiger's Milk bars found increasingly favorable rates of exchange. I had to trade away an entire half-pound of Tillamook cheese to secure three Diamox tablets. Adrian, who had an enviable hoard of food, was able to ease the interminable boredom by renting a Walkman from a hungry Canadian climber for the ridiculously low rate of one pemmican bar per day.

In the midst of those dark days I began to see Adrian's fiasco the year before in a different, more sympathetic light. I was forced to admit that on this, my first trip to Denali, I too had grossly underestimated the mountain. I had listened to the rangers' warnings; I had heard no less experienced an alpinist than Peter Habeler pronounce that McKinley's storms "are some of the worst I have ever experienced"; I knew that when Dougal Haston and Doug Scott had climbed McKinley together just six months after standing upon the summit of Everest, Haston had said they'd been forced to draw "on all our Himalayan experience just to survive." And yet, somehow—like Adrian in 1986—I hadn't really believed any of it. This was reflected in the corners I'd cut: I'd brought along a pitiful ten-year-old sleeping bag and a bargain-basement tent, and had neglected to pack a down jacket, overboots, a snow saw, or any snow pickets. I figured the West Buttress to be a farmer's route; I mean, how challenging could a climb that succumbed to three hundred freds and hackers a year possibly be?

Plenty challenging for the likes of me, it transpired. I was continually miserable, and frequently on the brink of disaster. My tent was starting to shred even in the relative calm at 14,300. The unceasing cold caused my lips and fingers to crack and bleed; my feet were always numb. At night, even wearing every article of clothing I had, it was impossible to stave off violent shivering attacks. Condensed breath would build up an inch of frost on the inside of my tent, creating an ongoing indoor blizzard as the gossamer nylon walls rattled in the wind. Anything not stowed inside my sleeping bag—camera, sunscreen, water bottles, stove—would freeze into a useless, brittle brick. My stove did in fact self-destruct from the cold early in the trip; had a kind soul named Brian Sullivan not taken pity on me and lent me his spare, I would—as Dick Danger so eloquently put it—have been in deep shit.

The storm reached a new level of violence on the morning of May 21. That evening, however—despite a forecast of high winds and heavy snowfall for at least five more days—the sky cleared and the wind quit. By the following morning it was thirty below and a few small lenticular clouds had reappeared over the summit of Foraker, but it was still calm and otherwise clear, so I packed a light rucksack and accepted an invitation to join a strong five-man party led by Tom Hargis—a Himalayan veteran who had made the second ascent of notorious Gasherbrum IV in 1986—to attempt a one-day, six-thousand-foot push for the summit. As I pulled out of camp, Adrian took a look at the sky, let out a cackle, and yelled, "Good luck, dude! You sure going to need it! I think maybe I find you up there later, frozen like fish!"

By the time we reached the start of the knife-edge ridge at 16,200 feet, two hours after setting out, the breeze had risen to twenty knots and clouds were starting to obscure the sun. Upon reaching 17,000 feet, an hour later, we were climbing in a full-blown blizzard, with near-zero visibility and a forty-knot wind that froze exposed flesh in seconds. At that point Hargis, who was in the lead, quietly did an about-face and headed down, and nobody questioned the decision. After surviving the West Ridge of Everest and Gasherbrum IV, Hargis was apparently not interested in buying the farm in pursuit of the Butt.

With the return of the storm on the twenty-second, the Honeymooners finally threw in the towel. That afternoon they stumbled into camp at 14,300 feet, completely whipped but with an astounding bit of news: The strange guys in the cave had made the summit.

One by one, other parties had gradually abandoned their fortified encampments at 17,200, but Dick and the Members had hung tough. Further excavations in their shelter had revealed just enough old cached food—some ancient but edible oatmeal, a little chocolate, a can of tuna and another of kippered herring—to sustain them. When their stove had started to malfunction, they mooched

△ 79

melted snow to drink from their original cavemates, the 5150 expedition.

5150 was a team of four Alaskans who took their name from the state penal code (5150, in copspeak, is the designation for "people of unsound mind"), and their inspiration from regular inhalations of Matanuska Thunderfuck, a legendary strain of *Cannabis sativa* cultivated in the forty-ninth state. The 5150 crew boasted, in fact, that they had consumed more than a hundred joints of the potent weed between Kahiltna International and 17,200. Even this prodigious chemical fortification, however, was not enough to prevent one member from becoming extremely hypothermic after only a day in the ice cave, so his teammates attempted to revive him by upping his intake further still. "It was kind of pathetic," Mike Dagon says. "They kept telling him, 'It's gotten you this far, it can get you the rest of the way, too.' But when the guy still hadn't warmed up after two days in the cave, the 5150 boys decided to make a break for it and bailed out."

The departure of 5150 and their functioning stove might have had dire consequences for the Members, but no sooner had 5150 moved out than the Crack o'Noon Club moved in. The Nooners also proved to have a working cooker, and were no less generous about sharing the water it produced.

"Mornings in the cave," Dagon admits, "were real depressing. I mean, you'd wake up and some guy'd be snoring in your face, there'd be nothing to eat, and all you had to look forward to was another day of staring at each other in an ice hole. But we managed to keep it together pretty well. To kill time we played trivia games, or talked about the food we were going to eat when we got down, and Este taught us the theme songs from shows like 'Gilligan's Island' and 'I Dream of Jeannie.' "

Then, on the evening of May 21, the gale suddenly abated. Dick and the Members were frostbitten, severely dehydrated, weak from hunger, stupid from the altitude, and sick from breathing the carbon monoxide put off by their stove. But they also subscribed to the

△ 80

"no guts, no glory" school of alpinism, and figured the mountain might not see clear skies again for another month. They did their best to ignore their infirmities, and all but Greg Siewers—the only experienced climber among them—mobilized to make an assault on the summit. At 9:30 P.M., in the company of the Crack o'Noon Club, they emerged from their icy burrow and started upward.

The Members moved painfully slowly in the bitter night air, and were soon left behind by the three Crack o'Nooners. At 18,500 feet, just after midnight, one of Dagon's mechanical ascenders broke while he was using it on a short piece of fixed line, and when he took his mitten off to try to fix the ascender, the mitten blew away. A few minutes later, Yates felt a tug on the rope and turned around. "Mike told me his hand was cold," Yates recalls, "and I looked down and saw that it was bare, but Mike didn't seem to realize it. I didn't know how long it had been like that, but I could see he was in trouble and starting to lose it bad. I immediately took his hand and shoved it inside my jacket."

When Dagon's hand had warmed up, a spare mitten was produced, and the Members continued upward until 5:30 A.M., at which time they'd reached the base of the final headwall at 19,000 feet. There, they had to stop again, this time for a full hour, to warm Dagon's hands and feet on Yates's and Parker's bellies. "Este told Mike that he was going seriously hypothermic, that we should go down," says Yates, "but Mike said no way, not when we were that close, and he reached deep and found the strength to keep going up the last thousand feet."

As they made their way up the summit ridge, they could see the graceful spires of Mt. Huntington and the Mooses Tooth poking surrealistically out of a thick layer of clouds blanketing the Ruth Glacier, a distant thirteen thousand feet below. "I knew in an abstract, intellectual sort of way," Yates explains, "that it was a beautiful view, but I couldn't get myself to care about it: I'd been up all night; I felt totally strung out; I was just too tired."

At 9:20 on the morning of May 22, 1987, the Members finally

△ 81

stood on the summit of McKinley. The pinnacle of North America, Mike Dagon reports, consists "of three insignificant bumps on a rounded ridge, with one bump rising a little higher than the others. That's all. It was incredibly anticlimactic; I guess I expected there to be fireworks, and music playing in my head or something, but there wasn't anything like that. As soon as we got there we turned around and started down."

Within minutes after the Members topped out, the layer of clouds they'd first seen hovering over the Ruth had climbed the thirteen thousand feet to summit: the sixteen-hour window of good weather had slammed shut. For the next six hours they fought their way through a whiteout to 17,200. Only a trail of bamboo tomato stakes, stuck into the snow every rope-length on the way up by the Crack o'Nooners, enabled the Members to make it back to their cave, which they did after eighteen straight hours of climbing. Once in the cave, the Members were pinned down by the weather for two more foodless days, but on May 24 they finally managed to drag themselves down to 14,300, where Rob Roach and Howard Donner attended to their frozen digits in the medical tent for several hours.

By demonstrating what could be achieved with bullheaded determination and a high pain threshold, the Members—one of only a handful of expeditions to make the summit in May—should have inspired the rest of us at 14,300 to suck it in a little harder and take our own best shot at greatness. By then, however, I was running low on Fig Newtons, and had developed a powerful thirst for something with more kick to it than melted snow. On May 26 I packed my tent, locked down my ski bindings, and bid my comrades in arms adieu.

As I shouldered my pack to go, Adrian looked wistfully off to the south toward Talkeetna, and started muttering about how the weather didn't really look like it was going to improve any time soon. "Maybe," he thought out loud, "the best thing is for me to go down like you, climb McKinley next year instead." But a moment later he turned his gaze back toward the peak and set his jaw. As I poled off down the glacier, Adrian was still standing there, staring up at the summit slopes, conjuring up images, I have no doubt, of the glories awaiting the first Romanian to climb Mc-Kinley.

7. CHAMONIX

IT'S ONLY SEPTEMBER, BUT THE WIND SMELLS LIKE WINTER AS IT GUSTS through the narrow streets of Chamonix, France. Each night the snow line, like the hem of a slip, pushes farther down the ample granite hips of Mont Blanc toward the stubble of slate roofs and church steeples on the valley floor. Three weeks ago the sidewalk cafes along the Avenue Michel Croz were choked with vacationers sipping overpriced *citron* and craning their necks at the famous skyline, two vertical miles above their tables and shimmering like a mirage in the August haze. Now most of those same cafes are empty, the hotels deserted, the recently throbbing bistros quiet as libraries. Wandering Chamonix's streets a few minutes before midnight, I am therefore surprised to see a crowd queued up outside the entrance to *Choucas*, a nightclub near the center of town. Curious, I fall in at the end of the line.

Twenty-five minutes later, finally inside, it's standing room only. Elvis Costello is thundering over the sound system with sufficient wattage to rattle the beer glasses, and it's impossible to see from one end of the bar to the other through the blue fog of smoldering *Gitanes*. The youthful clientele possesses a cocky, self-absorbed allure that brings to mind Shakespeare's line about "the confident and over-lusty French," but there is no dancing; surprisingly few people appear to be on the prowl; hardly anyone is even engaged in conversation. The patrons of *Choucas*, I deduce soon enough, come strictly for the videos: Every face in the joint is glued to the club's half-dozen giant television screens, transfixed by the flicker of the cathode rays.

▲ 84

The video presently mesmerizing the crowd depicts a popular French activity called "bungee jumping." A tall, striking blonde named Isabelle Patissier has ascended several thousand feet above the countryside in a hot air balloon. One end of a hundred-foot rubber band is knotted around the Frenchwoman's ankles, the other end is attached to the basket of the balloon. Patissier—one of the world's best rock climbers, and no shrinking violet—calmly executes a swan dive from the lip of the basket and into the void. She accelerates earthward at an alarming clip, but the rubber band breaks the fall successfully, bringing her to a spectacular, high-bouncing stop; Patissier, however, is unable to shinny back up the bungee cord to the security of the balloon, and is left dangling upside down in the breeze. To rectify the situation, the pilot of the balloon attempts an emergency landing, but in so doing he entangles the bungee cord in a high-voltage power line, nearly electrocuting Patissier, who is still hanging helplessly by her feet at the business end of the rubber band, which has by now caught fire.

Patissier is ultimately snatched from the jaws of death, but before anyone in the bar can take a deep breath the screen cuts to another, equally gripping video, this one about a local hero, Christophe Profit, solo-climbing the Walker Spur, the Eigerwand, and the North Face of the Matterhorn, all in the space of a single winter's day. The entertainment continues in this vein until closing time, with tapes of wing-walking, nude sky diving, big-wave surfing, high-speed mono-skiing down a slope of pumice, Evel-Knievel-like motorcycle stunts. The common thread running through all the videos is mortal risk; the grimmer things get, the more rapt the crowd becomes. Indeed, the most popular tape of all is a forty-five-minute compilation of fatal Grand Prix automobile crashes, a grisly smorgasbord of drivers and spectators being crushed, dismembered, and burned alive—the lot of it enhanced for our viewing pleasure with full-frame close-ups and replays in super slo-mo.

At one point in the evening there is some sort of snafu with the video machine, the screens go blank, and I find myself chatting with a young Frenchman from the nearby city of Annecy. Patrick is attired in calf-length floral-print beach trousers, an oversize Batman sweatshirt, and—never mind that the sun set some six hours ago and we are in a dimly lit bar besides—a pair of pink-framed glacier glasses. He allows with characteristic Gallic modesty that he is both an expert *parapente* pilot and a "superbe" rock climber. I respond that I, too, happen to be a climber, and that I've been quite pleased with the quality of the routes I've completed in Chamonix thus far; seizing the opportunity to do some chest-thumping of my own, I go on to tell Patrick that I especially enjoyed the route I'd done just the day before, a classic test piece—rated *extrêmement difficile* in the Vallot guidebook—on a slender, improbably steep spire called the Grand Capucin.

"The Capucin?" replies Patrick, clearly impressed. "That must have been a very difficult summit to launch the *parapente* from, yes?" No, no, I quickly interject—I simply climbed the peak; I didn't mean to suggest that I'd also flown off it. "Non?" says Patrick, momentarily taken aback. "Well, to solo the Capucin, that is a worthwhile undertaking all the same." Actually, I sheepishly explain, I hadn't soloed the peak, either: I'd done it with a partner and a rope. "You did not solo and you did not fly?" asks the Frenchman, incredulous. "Did you not find the experience a little—how you say in English—*banal*?"

In stumbling upon *Choucas*, I was later informed, I'd inadvertently discovered the hippest bistro in Chamonix. Which was saying something, because Chamonix, though populated by fewer than eleven thousand year-round residents, has for two centuries been the hippest mountain community on the Continent, maybe the entire planet, and not merely in the minds of those who live there. Chamonix, understand, is considerably more than the Aspen of the Alps; it's the very birthplace of *haute chic*. It's no accident that when

Yvon Chouinard wanted to establish a maximally visible retail beachhead on the far side of the Atlantic, the first Patagonia store he opened in Europe was in downtown Chamonix.

Chamonix proper is overbuilt and not particularly handsome by European architectural standards. There are too many tourist traps, too many megalithic concrete eyesores, far too many cars and nowhere at all to put them. All the same, enough Old World remains in the town's twisting cobbled streets and ancient, thick-walled chalets to make even the most appealing American ski towns seem pseudo-Bavarian theme parks by comparison. Jammed into the cramped, claustrophobically narrow valley of the River Arve, just eight miles from the point where Italy, Switzerland, and France share a common frontier, the community is hemmed in hard to the north by the 9,000-foot peaks of the Aiguilles Rouges and even harder to the south by the 15,771-foot mass of Mont Blanc. The highest point in western Europe, it towers so near at hand that paragliders routinely touch down in the village center after taking off from the mountain's summit.

The popularity of *Choucas*'s eclectic video fare isn't surprising: the lifeblood of the entire town, after all, is high-risk recreation and the marketing thereof. As American alpinist Marc Twight—who has been living here intermittently for the past five years—says with great affection and tongue only partially in cheek, Chamonix is nothing less than the "death sport capital of the world." The huge billboard that greets visitors as they motor into Chamonix on the main highway from Italy claims only that they have arrived in the *"Capitale Mondiale du Ski et Alpinisme"*—the World Capital of Skiing and Climbing. And lo, the sign does not exaggerate, for Chamonix and Chamoniards are at the cutting edge of international climbing, perhaps now more than ever before. But in the frenetic, adrenaline-besotted climate of the past decade, Twight's sobriquet has come to seem the more accurate of the two. The impeccably creased knickers and classic guides' sweaters of old have been sup-

△ 87

planted by neon-hued Lycra and Gore-tex, and traditional mountaineering has mutated here into a host of alpine thrill sports that Dr. Paccard would be hard put to recognize.

Dr. Michel-Gabriel Paccard, you'll recall, invented the sport of mountain climbing on August 8, 1786, by making the first ascent of Mont Blanc, in the company of a local chamois hunter named Jacques Balmat. Following the ordeal, Balmat reported, "my eyes were red, my face black and my lips blue. Everytime I laughed or yawned the blood spouted from my lips and cheeks, and, in addition, I was half-blind." For their inestimable contribution to the future economic base of the community, the two original alpinists received a cash prize of what amounted to sixty U.S. dollars, the village center was designated *Place Balmat*, and the town's main drag was christened the *Rue du Dr. Paccard*—along which, two centuries later, you will find not only *Choucas* and the spiffy new Patagonia store, but merchants selling everything from paragliders, Parisian lingerie, and postcards of climbing stars Jean-Marc Boivin and Catherine Destivelle, to graphite-shafted ice axes, titanium pitons, and state-of-the-art snowboards embossed with likenesses of the Manhattan skyline.

In the decades following the Paccard-Balmat climb, as accounts of that deed and subsequent ascents circulated across the Continent, Chamonix became an exceedingly fashionable destination for the rich and famous, and rapidly developed into the world's first mountain resort (previously, as *New Yorker* writer Jeremy Bernstein has pointed out, mountains were generally regarded as "terrifying, ugly, and an obstacle to travel and commerce, and anyone living in or near them as subhuman"). Goethe, Byron, Ruskin, Percy Shelley, the Prince of Wales, and ex-Empress Josephine all sojourned there. By 1876, 795 men and women had reached the top of Mont Blanc, among them an Englishman named Albert Smith who passed out drunk on the summit after he and his companions put away ninety-six bottles of wine, champagne, and cognac in the course of their ascent.

As the heavy traffic on Mont Blanc began to rob the climb of its cachet (by its easiest routes, the 15,771-foot peak is not technically demanding or even very steep), ambitious alpinists turned their attention to the hundreds of sheer-walled satellite peaks—the fabled Chamonix Aiguilles—that stud the ridges of the massif like the spines of a stegosaur. In 1881, when Albert Mummery, Alexander Burgener, and Benedict Venetz bagged the fearsome-looking Aiguille du Grepon, it was lauded as a superhuman feat. Nevertheless, in a prescient moment following the climb, Mummery predicted that it would only be a matter of time before the Grepon lost its reputation as "the most difficult ascent in the Alps" and came to be regarded as "an easy day for a lady."

A hundred years after Mummery's heyday, new techniques, better equipment, and a population explosion on the heights have brought about just the sort of devaluation Mummery feared, not only of the Grepon, but of most of the other "last great problems" that followed: the Walker Spur, the Freney Pillar, the North Face of Les Droites, the Dru Couloir, to name but a few.

Although Mont Blanc is a mountain of genuinely Himalayan proportions, boasting an uninterrupted vertical rise of nearly thirteen thousand feet from base to summit, it also happens to sit squarely in the teeming lap of western Europe, and therein lies the rub. It's this unlikely juxtaposition of radical topography and rarefied Continental culture that, for better and worse, begat modern Chamonix.

On a nice summer day, the streets will be peopled with a mix you'd expect to find in any French tourist town: mink-wrapped matrons, tourists from Cincinnati and Milan, frail old men in wool berets, leggy shop girls in black hose and miniskirts. What's different about Cham—as the village is termed in the local patois—is that fully half the people walking past will be clomping along in climbing boots and have a coil of 8.8-millimeter perlon slung over a shoulder. And if you watch long enough, sooner or later you might see Boivin, or Profit, or Marc Batard stroll past, *heros de la*

République all, whose exploits are regularly reported in the pages of large-circulation magazines like *Paris-Match*. Last year Boivin became the first man to fly a paraglider from the summit of Everest, his rival Batard became the first to ascend the same mountain in less than a day, and, in a coup that many French consider most impressive of all, Profit climbed the long, savage knife-edge of Mont Blanc's Peuterey Ridge, alone and in winter, in nineteen hours flat.

When Profit or, say, world champion mono-skier Eric Saerens is spotted in a Chamonix restaurant, it sets the place abuzz in the same way that the presence of Mattingly or Magic Johnson would in the States. The French, it goes without saying, are far too urbane to fawn over their luminaries in public like we do. But there are exceptions: When rock climbing superstar Patrick Edlinger comes to town, says Twight, "everybody slobbers over him shamelessly. Two winters ago I went to a party at *Choucas* where Edlinger was in attendance, and it was like he was holding court. People were practically fighting each other for the chance to get to his table and pay homage."

Not that all the alpinists in Cham are stars. Mont Blanc is now climbed by nearly six thousand people every year, and tens of thousands of others swarm over the adjacent Aiguilles. A *million* thrill chasers of one kind or another pass through Chamonix annually. The massif is encircled with hotels, peppered with multi-story "huts," crisscrossed by fifty-seven chair lifts and aerial trams, and pierced by a seven-mile tunnel through which runs a major European highway. At the apogee of climbing season the Vallee Blanche—the high glacial plateau that feeds the Mer de Glace—is crowded with so many alpinists that from the air it bears an uncanny resemblance to an ant colony. The number of new climbing routes documented in the record books of the Office de Haute Montagne is mind-addling; there's scarcely a square meter of rock or ice left in the entire range that hasn't been ascended by somebody.

One might conclude that every last ounce of challenge has long since been wrung from the mountains above Chamonix, but one would be wrong. The French, being a proud and creative people with a gift for self-dramatization, have had little trouble finding novel forms of alpine stimulation. In addition to the obvious variations—speed climbing, extreme solo climbing, extreme skiing—they have fervently embraced such activities as bungee jumping, *le surf extrem* (extreme snowboarding), *le ski sur herbe* (using wheeled skis to rocket down grassy summer slopes), *ballule* rolling (careering downhill inside giant inflatable balls), and—the most popular new game of all—flying off mountaintops with paragliders, which the French call *parapentes*.

It's a luminous fall afternoon in downtown Cham, and I'm sitting on the terrace of the *Brasserie L'M*, loitering over a strawberry crêpe and a café au lait, wondering whether I might, given my limited talents, ever rise above the life of the terminally banal. Overhead, a nonstop parade of paragliders is floating across the sky, en route from one or another of the surrounding alps to a meadow a few blocks away that serves as the town landing field. When I finally get tired of the waiter inquiring every few minutes if I'll be having anything else ("Or will monsieur be leaving now?"), I get up and walk to the meadow, which lies at the base of the Brevent ski lift, to catch a little flying action at close range.

In all of the United States, there are at most four hundred paraglider pilots, a number that reflects the sport's reputation for being insanely dangerous. (Evincing a firm commitment to truth in advertising, the leading U.S. manufacturer of paragliders—Feral, Inc.—has for its corporate logo a skull and crossbones.) Neither mortal risk nor fear of litigation, however, has slowed the proliferation of paragliding in the Alps: At last count there were an estimated twelve thousand parapilots at large in France. And the zeal with which the French have taken up paragliding has nothing to do with some Gallic knack for avoiding accidents: Parapilots in Chamonix are forever crashing onto rooftops and busy highways, being blown into ski lifts, and dropping out of the sky like flies.

△ 91

Indeed, within half an hour of my arrival at the Chamonix landing field, I witness two paragliders overshoot the tiny meadow and plow into the trees, and see a third slam face-first into the second-story wall of an apartment building.

The swelling tally of paragliding mishaps, however, is unlikely to move the French to ban the sport from their ski resorts (as Americans have), nor is the annual carnage from climbing ever likely to lead to the curtailment of that activity. This despite the fact that between forty and sixty people come to unpleasant ends in the mountains above Chamonix in a typical year, and that the overall body count on Mont Blanc now totals more than two thousand, making it far and away the deadliest mountain on earth.

Interestingly enough, routine, lift-served skiing—an activity that few American practitioners think of as life-threatening—contributes to approximately half the annual death toll. There are eight ski areas in the Chamonix Valley, and their slopes include many runs that are no more challenging than the tamest trails at Stowe or Park City, but there is also a vast amount of lift-served terrain that blurs the line between ordinary skiing and hard-core mountaineering. Take a wrong turn, for instance, when you get off the lift on the Grands Montets or the Aiguille du Midi—two of the most popular places to ski—and you could easily wind up in the bottom of a crevasse, or buried under avalanching seracs, or skidding off a thousand-foot cliff. In the United States, skiers take it for granted that natural hazards, if they exist at all, will be carefully fenced off, marked with signs, or otherwise rendered idiot-proof. In Chamonix personal safety is rightly seen as the responsibility of the skier, not the ski area, and idiots don't last long.

The French, when it comes right down to it, look at risky sports—and sports in general—in a fundamentally different way than Americans do. We go in for team sports like baseball and football, and the athletic heroes we hold up for our kids to emulate tend to be cast in the squeaky-clean Orel Hershiser mold. The French, in marked contrast, are notorious individualists with a fondness for the sensational deed, the stylish twist, the dramatic solitary act; their athletic role models tend to chain-smoke *Gitanes*, drive irresponsibly fast, and excel at activities like long-distance windsurfing or soloing 5.12 rock climbs.

And so, Chamoniards may not be happy about all the bloodshed that occurs in their backyard, but they are adept at shrugging it off. "In Chamonix," a wiry thirty-year-old *gendarme* named Luc Bellon explained to me, "there is a special mind. Maybe you are not a guide or a climber—maybe you are a butcher or own a souvenir shop—it makes no difference, the mountains still put food on your table. Like fishermen with the sea, we have learned to accept the danger and the tragedies as a fact of life here."

Although Luc Bellon works as a *gendarme*—a French cop—it should not be inferred that he spends his days arresting pickpockets or directing traffic in a silly pillbox cap. Bellon, rather, belongs to an elite arm of the state police called the *Peloton de Gendarmerie de Haute Montagne*, PGHM for short, whose job it is to bail out those hapless adventurers who find more excitement than they reckoned on. The *Thwock! Thwock! Thwock!* of a squat blue PGHM helicopter, speeding off toward the Aiguilles to retrieve another broken body from the heights, is as common over Chamonix as is the sound of police sirens in the Bronx: In July and August, when the glaciers and Aiguilles are mobbed with incautious alpinists from around the world, Bellon and his cohorts are frequently called on to perform ten or fifteen rescues or body recoveries a day.

Ironically, the skill and vigilance of the PGHM may actually add to the astounding number of accidents in Chamonix, for many would-be Boivins take even greater chances than they normally would, knowing that Bellon and company are standing by 'round the clock to save their bacon. According to John Bouchard, an accomplished American alpinist who has been coming to Chamonix since 1973 (and who with his French wife owns Wild Things, the climbing gear company, and Feral, of the skull-and-crossbones paragliders), "These days, instead of taking emergency bivouac

△ 93

gear, guys go out on hard climbs and take nothing but a radio. If things get sketchy they assume they can just get on the horn and call for a rescue."

I confess to contemplating a similar gambit myself during my visit last fall. On my second day in Cham, I set out alone up a steep but oft-ascended groove of ice on a 13,937-foot peak called Mont Blanc du Tacul. Low on the climb, I repeatedly struck rock as I slammed my ice axes through the couloir's thin glazing, carelessly dulling the picks; by the time I was midway up the route, being both unacclimated and badly out of shape, I began to have difficulty swinging the blunt tools hard enough to make them stick. Since I hadn't brought along a rope for rappeling down, however, my only option appeared to be to continue front-pointing the rest of the way to the top and walk down the easy backside. Just then a PGHM helicopter buzzed past on a routine flight, and, spying me, hovered to determine whether or not they'd come across another bonehead in trouble. Immediately, I decided to wave for help. Only the day before, after all, I'd plunked down seventy dollars for rescue insurance, so the impromptu extrication wouldn't cost me a dime.

Problem was, I couldn't figure what sort of story I was going to give to the PGHM to justify the rescue when the guy in the natty blue sweater came down on the winch cable to pluck me from the ice. I hesitated for a moment, then, overcome with guilt, raised one arm—the signal that all was well—and the chopper darted off toward the valley like an overgrown dragonfly, leaving me to my own sorry devices.

Among the thousands of lurid mishaps and stirring rescues that have occurred in Chamonix over the years, a few stand out. The most famous rescue of them all occurred in the summer of 1966 on the west face of the Petit Dru, an arresting granite obelisk that soars six thousand feet above the Mer de Glace. Two inexperienced Germans had started up the wall on August 14, and after four days of climbing became marooned on a three-foot ledge, two-thirds of the way to the top, unable to surmount the ice-plastered overhangs that guard the summit pinnacle. The Germans sent out an SOS, hunkered down on their tiny ledge, and waited for help as bad weather closed in.

A massive rescue effort was set in motion. More than fifty French Mountain Troops and Chamonix guides ascended the less difficult north and east faces of the Dru, and attempted to lower a steel cable from the summit. The overhangs directly above the stranded climbers, however, repeatedly foiled this scheme, and three days after the signal for help went out, the Germans were still out of reach. By then Chamonix was flooded with reporters and television crews, and the rescue was front-page news in every major paper in western Europe.

Gary Hemming read about the plight of the Germans on August 18, while sitting in a cafe on the Italian side of Mont Blanc, and decided straightaway that he was the man to save them. Hemming—a tall, dreamy Californian with shaggy blonde hair and bohemian inclinations—had been residing in France for five years, mostly in Chamonix but occasionally in Paris as well, where he slept under bridges by the Seine. Three years later, for reasons that are still puzzled over, Hemming would get drunk in a Teton campground and put a bullet through his own head, but in 1966 the thirty-three-year-old climber was at the top of his game.

Hemming had been on the west face of the Dru many times; in 1962 he and Royal Robbins had pioneered a new route on the wall, the "American Direct," that at the time was considered one of the world's hardest climbs, and is still regarded as one of the great lines in the Alps. As a consequence, Hemming knew the mountain intimately, and when he read about the Germans' predicament, he quickly concluded that the best way to save them was to climb the west face itself, a course of action that both the military rescuers and the strongest guides in Chamonix had dismissed as impossible, given the stormy weather and the icy condition of the wall. Hem-

△ 95

ming raced back to Chamonix and started up the west face on August 19, leading an ad hoc, multinational team that eventually came to number eight renegade climbers.

The climbing was unspeakably hard, but after three days Hemming's party reached the Germans' ledge to find the two men alive and in surprisingly good shape. Incredibly, five minutes later, one of the guides from the north face team arrived on the scene as well, having made a circuitous traverse from the easier route, and announced that he and the other guides would now be evacuating the Germans. "No," Hemming is said to have replied with feeling. "We got here first. The Germans are ours."

A day later, Hemming's team completed their descent with the Germans safely in tow to find the assembled media waiting for them at the base of the Dru with cameras and tape recorders rolling. When Hemming's contemplative visage and stirring tale landed in the papers and on the TV screens of Europe, he became the toast of the Continent. The French, especially, went gaga over "le Beatnik," this noble savage from America with the rugged good looks and Gary-Cooper-like reticence. Hemming was suddenly a hero, transformed overnight from a penniless, maladjusted climber into a perfect blonde god, and launched into enduring myth.

"There is no easy way into another world," writes James Salter in *Solo Faces*, the spare, powerful novel he set in Chamonix and based loosely on the life of Hemming. Chamoniards are an exceedingly insular people, disinclined to open their lives to outsiders. Many of the surnames one sees above the shops on the *Rue du Dr. Paccard* or on the roster at the Guides Bureau—Balmat, Payot, Simond, Charlet, Tournier, Devouassoud—have been there since Goethe and Empress Josephine first came to town. Indeed, no "outsiders"—which Chamoniards define as anyone born more than a few kilometers beyond the town limits—are accepted into the ranks of the *Compagnie des Guides de Chamonix Mont-Blanc* without a special, seldom-granted dispensation. A band of young, "foreign-born" (i.e., non-Chamoniard) guides has retaliated by forming a competing service, *Les Guides Independant du Mont Blanc*, but in the eyes of most Chamoniards the freelancers are to the established *Compagnie* what a jug of Gallo is to vintage Chateau Lafite-Rothschild.

Hemming managed to penetrate Cham's closed society only after his heroics on the Dru (the French have always had a deep and abiding respect for fame). John Bouchard was eventually embraced by the Chamoniards, too, but not until he completed a string of brilliant, unthinkably bold ascents—two of them on previously unclimbed routes; several of them done alone—that culminated in his marriage to Titoune Meunier, an extraordinary climber herself, who is a member of the local Simond clan. According to Marc Twight, Bouchard's friend and protege, "John went to Cham, snatched these coveted first ascents away from the heaviest hitters in the Alps, and then stole the heart of the most desirable girl in town." It was just the sort of tour de force, executed with consummate style, that the French find irresistible. From that point on Chamoniards regarded Bouchard as one of their own, a native son who by some inexplicable cosmic accident happened to have been born in America.

Beyond Hemming and Bouchard, however, precious few Americans—or foreigners of any stripe, for that matter—have ever been admitted to the club. Marc Twight—an intense, very talented twenty-eight-year-old alpinist—is a case in point. Over the past five years Twight has polished off a horrific list of infamous Chamonix "death routes," and last March was the subject of a ten-page spread in *Montagnes*, the French climbing magazine. But he still does not feel accepted, really, by the locals. "When I first arrived here in 1984," he says, "I was basically shunned and ignored. Now that I've done some good climbs, the hot local climbers and para-pilots will let me into their periphery, talk to me, share info about routes. But that's all you get. You still aren't invited over for dinner; you'll never be admitted to the inner circle. I'm not sure why; that's just the way it is."

Most foreign climbers and skiers—the legions of Basques, Brits, Czechs, Poles, Germans, Swedes, Italians, Spaniards, Argentines, Americans, Koreans, Canadians, Australians, Norwegians, New Zealanders, Indians, and Japanese who flock to Chamonix annually—could care less about gaining entrance to Chamonix society; they aspire only to be left alone, to roll the dice on the heights as the spirit moves them, and to get by as cheaply and comfortably as possible in the valley between epics.

As one might imagine, with such a wide range of nationalities, an equally wide range of strategies has been adopted to achieve these ends. The Czechs and Poles, for instance, who tend to be both short of hard currency and hard as nails, eschew the hotels and *pensions* in favor of farmers' fields on the outskirts of town, where they pay four or five francs per night for the privilege of shitting in the woods and pitching their ragged tents amid the mud and cow pies.

Likewise, few Swedes will be found in Chamonix hotels, although for a different reason. In Sweden, it seems, there is a prohibitively stiff tax on alcohol. When Swedes come to France, where booze costs approximately half what it does in Scandinavia, they are apt to overindulge, and, as Twight puts it, "get wicked out of control. They start fights, trash rooms, and become extremely unruly. As a result, when Chamoniard innkeepers see a Swedish passport they usually say, 'I am sorry, but I just remembered that all the rooms are already taken.' " Things have degenerated to the point where Swedish businessmen recently bought some hotels in the village of Argentiere, a few miles up the valley, just so their countrymen would have a place near Chamonix to sleep; nowadays, during ski season, Argentiere turns into a veritable Swedish colony.

Even touchier than Franco-Swedish relations, however, are those between the French and the British, thanks to a mutual enmity that has been festering for so many centuries that it's been encoded in the respective parties' genes. The Brits do have one or two allies among the Chamoniards: The local Snell clan has for three decades allowed Englishmen, by tacit agreement, to camp in a family-owned field at the edge of town in return for not ripping off the two family-owned climbing shops on the *Rue du Dr. Paccard*. But the bad blood between many French and British alpinists runs deep nevertheless, and has on occasion escalated into legendary brawls that have devastated bistros and landed a number of famous English climbers in the Chamonix jail.

The bad blood is also reflected in Franco-English slang. To the English, for instance, a condom is a "French letter"; to the French it's "*une capote anglais*." When someone sneaks away dishonorably the Brits refer to it as "taking French leave"; the French say "*filer à l'anglais*." In colloquial French, sodomy is known as "*le vice anglais*," and although the English in this case lack a precise etymological equivalent, British climbers have long considered the sartorial flair of their Gallic counterparts to be proof positive that all Frenchmen are latent deviants.

Lately, however, the French have seemed to be enjoying the last laugh. These days the native Chamoniards are not only the best-dressed climbers, skiers, and parapilots on the hill, but for the first time since the Paccard-Balmat climb there isn't an Englishman (or anyone else) alive who can match their astonishing poise and prowess on severe ice and rock. Superstars like Profit, Boivin, and Patrick Gabarrou might have a weakness for pink scarves and color-coordinated alpine ensembles, but nobody's calling them weenies.

It takes about half an hour for the two-stage *téléphérique* to travel the nine thousand vertical feet between Chamonix and the summit of the Aiguille du Midi. Sixty of us have been shoehorned into the rusty box of the cable car for the ride up: Frenchmen in fluorescent orange-and-green outfits with matching backpacks; several teams from an Italian climbing club, singing and farting and laughing

△ 99

enthusiastically; a few silent Japanese tourists incongruously attired in business suits and dresses.

At the summit—a dizzying spike of brown granite, honeycombed with tunnels and barnacled with bizarre steel structures—I find my way to the restaurant for a quick *croque-monsieur*, then board another lift for a ride across the heavily crevassed plain of the Vallee Blanche to the Italian frontier. From there, a short downhill walk takes me to my objective for the day, the north face of a peak called the Tour Ronde. Were this mountain in Alaska, where I have done much of my climbing, I might have spent three or four days laboring beneath an eighty-pound pack to arrive at this point from the Chamonix Valley. Because the peak is in France, the approach has taken me less than two hours (breakfast stop included), my rucksack holds little more than lunch and an extra sweater, and I haven't yet broken a sweat.

Were this peak in Alaska, however, I would probably have had it to myself; as I strap on my crampons at the foot of the Tour Ronde, I count seven climbers on the route above.

The climb follows an hourglass-shaped slab of glassy grey ice straight up for twelve hundred feet. By Chamonix standards the route is easy, but I'm concerned, nonetheless, about all the folks above me: In 1983, a pair of climbers fell near the top of the face, and as they plummeted to the glacier, still roped together, they flossed off eighteen people who had been climbing below, killing six and themselves.

The climbers overhead don't pose a problem until I reach the midway point on the wall, the waist of the hourglass, where rock buttresses on either side funnel all the ice kicked loose by those above down through a narrow slot, up which I must climb for two hundred feet. Fortunately, most of the ice chips whistling down are small and glance harmlessly off my helmet. Falling ice is to be expected on a climb like this—climbers can't help knocking off small divots when they drive in their axes—but for some incomprehensible reason one of the teams above begins sending down

△ 100

frisbees of granite, too, some of them weighing eight or ten pounds. "Hey!" I scream up in their direction. "Can't you see there's someone below you?" This, however, only seems to encourage them: When I turn my face upward to yell again, I catch a pebble in the chin. I quickly tuck my head back down and begin front-pointing even faster.

In ten minutes I'm out of the slot and onto the upper face, where it's possible to dodge the fusillade. Forty-five minutes after that I'm on top, where I find the two Frenchmen who rolled the rocks my way lounging beside the bronze statue of the Virgin Mary that marks the summit. Approaching them, I inquire politely, "What gives, assholes? On the descent maybe I should kick a few boulders down so you can see what it feels like."

The two climbers, who are in their early twenties, act supremely unconcerned. One of them shrugs and tells me, "The falling rocks, they are one of the many natural hazards climbers must face in the Alps. If you do not like the climbing here, perhaps you should return to America, where the mountains are not so big."

By and by, the Frenchmen depart, leaving me alone on the summit, and I begin to settle down. The rock is warm, the September sky crystalline and absolutely still. Around me, so close I can almost reach out and touch them, the Aiguilles rise in wave after endless wave. Here are the crest of Mont Blanc and the thin fingers of the Peuterey Ridge; over there, the Grepon and Charmoz, the immense tusk of the Dent du Geant, the twin summits of the Drus, the formidable profile of the Grandes Jorasses. For most of my life I've read about these peaks, stared at fuzzy photos of them clipped from magazines and scotch-taped to my walls, tried to imagine the texture of their storied granite.

It's getting late. I need to start climbing down, pronto, or I'll miss the last *téléphérique* to the valley. But there's a pleasant, peculiar sort of warmth inching up my spine, and I'm reluctant to cut it short before it has a chance to get wherever it may be going. "Five more minutes," I bargain with myself out loud. A quarter-mile

△ 101

beneath my feet, the shadow of the Tour Ronde stretches across the glacier like a cat.

When I glance at my watch, an hour has passed. Down in Chamonix, the streets are already deep in shade, and the bars are starting to fill with climbers and parapilots back from the heights. If I were down there now, sharing a table with some wild-eyed heir to Messner or Bonatti or Terray, my trip up the Tour Ronde would probably be too banal to mention. Up here on top of the mountain, my ledge affords a different perspective. The summits are still gleaming in the autumn sun. The walls are humming with history, the empty glacier is alive with light. "Five more minutes," I tell myself again. "Just five more minutes, and then I really will start down."

8. CANYONEERING

THE SALT RIVER SNAKES ACROSS THE MIDRIFF OF ARIZONA, FLOWING
west from the high Apache country near the New Mexico line,
down onto the scorched hardpan of the Sonoran Desert, and finally
through the smog and sprawl of Phoenix before surrendering both
its name and what remains of its waters to the Gila River. The Salt
has been so emasculated by dams, reservoirs, and irrigation canals
that, by the time it reaches downtown Phoenix, it's nothing more
than a sandy wash bounded by concrete embankments. When I
first laid eyes on the mighty Salt from the window of a 737 on final
approach to the Phoenix airport—on a day in early April, when
the stream was supposed to be running near full flow—there didn't
appear to be any water in the river at all.

Consequently, an hour later, when a fellow named Rick Fisher
earnestly informed me that the Salt was "one of the most spectacular
and challenging rivers in all of North America, and encompasses
one of the last true wilderness areas in the lower forty-eight states,"
I nodded politely and tried to cut the guy some slack by reminding
myself that I once attempted to convince a friend from Boston that
the Seattle Mariners—my hometown club, and perennial cellar
dwellers in the American League West—were in reality the most
talented team in baseball. Fisher, a thirty-six-year-old photographer
and backcountry guide from Tucson, picked up the skeptical look
in my eyes. "Just you wait," he smugly protested. "You'll see soon
enough."

But when we arrived in the canyon of the upper Salt to spend
a week poking around on the river and its tributaries, I still didn't

▲ 103

see. We were a hundred miles from Phoenix, above the last of the dams and diversion canals, so the river actually had water in it, and the parched country rising around us possessed a certain craggy charm, but few people would call the place spectacular, at least not by the inflated standards of a region that boasts Zion and the Grand Canyon a few hours up the road. Furthermore, some two hundred people—families in motor homes the size of battleships, party-hearty adolescents with boom boxes wailing, weekend river rats sporting forty-dollar haircuts and hundred-dollar shades, pink-faced good ol' boys knocking back beers—were camped along this stretch of riverbank, and a bumper-to-bumper parade of inflatable rafts bobbed past on the Salt's modest riffles from dawn til dusk. This canyon is plenty wild, I decided, but wilderness it ain't.

I had, however, closed the book on Fisher and the Salt too soon. Fisher turned out to have a knack for sniffing out pockets of the desert—some in the very shadow of the Sun Belt's thundering herds—that have somehow managed to duck the heavy hand of the twentieth century. A mile or two downstream from the crowded campground, Fisher parked his beat-up 4×4 and led four of his friends, two golden retrievers, and me up a narrow canyon of the main Salt cut by a creek called Cibecue.

Within minutes steep rock walls—a crazy mosaic of black vol-canic diabase and serpentine folds of yellow sandstone—began to press in overhead, and the floor of the defile grew so narrow that we had to wade directly up the knee-deep creek, the waters of which ran fast and clear and surprisingly cold. A half-mile up-stream, we rounded a bend to find ourselves in a natural cul de sac, a dramatic quirk of topography known in the local argot as a "rock box." Overhanging walls of polished stone surrounded us in a tight U-shaped grotto, with the whole of the creek spilling down from the head of this grotto in a free-falling fifty-foot torrent. Fur-ther progress up the canyon, it appeared, was going to demand some fairly interesting maneuvers, like unprotectable 5.12 face climbing in wet sneakers.

△ 104

Fortunately, it only appeared that way. Fisher directed us fifty yards back down the creek, where a rock pillar leaned halfway up against the east wall of the cliff. The pillar overhung its base slightly, but a greasy hand jam, a hidden "Thank God" hold, and an energetic mantleshelf led to the large ledge that capped the pillar; from there an easy scramble gained both the crest of the cliff and the whole of the upper canyon. In a few minutes all of us—including the dogs, who were strapped into makeshift harnesses and hauled up on a rope—were on top.

The climbing was not technically difficult, but, Fisher explained in the unhurried cadence and soft twang of the rural Southwest, "Ninety-eight percent of the folks who make it up the canyon this far, which isn't all that many folks to begin with, turn back because the box looks so intimidating." Fisher, a short, muscular man with a Pancho Villa moustache and a vaguely melancholy air, then confessed, "When I first started coming to this canyon the climbing was even easier, but a few years back some guys from Flagstaff brought in a hydraulic jack and pushed off this big block that used to lean up against the pillar, making it a lot less difficult to get to the top. I wouldn't have done something like that, but I guess I'm kind of glad they did. Thanks to the boys from Flag, only a few parties a year go beyond the falls. We're what, maybe half a mile from that zoo on the Salt, but from here on up the canyon's still pretty much like it was five hundred years ago."

Indeed, above the falls it felt like we'd entered an altogether different world. Even the vegetation was different: Because Cibecue Canyon is defended by formidable rock boxes at both its upper and lower ends, no cattle, horses, or sheep have ever found their way in. Consequently, the native riparian flora hasn't yet been displaced by cheat grass and other species that overwhelm the landscape where livestock graze.

As we moved up the canyon, it opened up into broad parklands for a mile or two, and then necked down once again into a deep, twisting slot that at one point was barely six feet across from wall

△ 105

to dead-vertical wall. We spied an eagle's nest balanced two hundred feet above the creek on the needle-like summit of a sandstone spire. Not far beyond the nest we passed beneath a cliff dwelling, still largely undisturbed, built seven hundred years ago by the Mogollon (pronounced MUGGY-un) people, enigmatic contemporaries of the Anasazi to the north.

Cibecue Creek, along with the Salt River and its other tributaries, drains the south slope of a landform known as the Mogollon Rim. The Rim, which slices diagonally across north-central Arizona between Flagstaff and Phoenix, marks the southern boundary of the enormous Colorado Plateau. With an abrupt 6,000-foot plunge in elevation, the Rim emphatically demarcates the high peaks and woodlands of the Rocky Mountains from the searing plains and basins of the Sonoran Desert.

The Rim is dotted with scores of small, ramshackle mining and ranching towns, and the lower reaches of its slope descend right to the periphery of greater Phoenix and the city's two million inhabitants. But because the lay of the Mogollon region is so severe, many of its ten-million-plus acres retain an aura of terra incognita and shelter a thriving population of black bears, bald and golden eagles, mountain lions, deer, and bighorn sheep. Fourteen or fifteen noteworthy canyons—sporting names like Salome Jug, Hell's Gate, Dry Beaver, Devil's Windpipe—corrugate the Rim's precipitous face, and, aside from visits by the odd rancher or prospector, have remained unexplored for centuries.

The charms of the Mogollon Rim were obscure enough that the Forest Service planned to offer the canyons up for commercial development in 1984; thankfully, this idea was nixed when a wilderness coalition, of which Fisher was a part, publicized the area and won protected status for it in Congress. This was a relief to Fisher, because to hear him talk, the Mogollon chasms present the finest canyoneering on the North American continent.

That's quite a claim. The Colorado River has chiseled a six-thousand-foot-deep, thousand-mile gash down the center of its namesake plateau, and each of the tributary streams that feed the Colorado—and each of the creeks and brooks that feed these tributary streams—has compounded this immense wound in the earth, transforming much of Colorado, Utah, Arizona, and New Mexico into a phantasmagoric labyrinth of red rock chasms. Literally hundreds of these canyons could be described as last great wild swatches of the lower forty-eight. Some have yet to be discovered; others exist as the province of only a few. How, then, in the name of John Wesley Powell, can anybody conclude that one, or two, or twenty particular canyons are somehow better than the rest?

To understand why Fisher insists that the Mogollon canyons— most of which are all but unknown even within the borders of Arizona—are more worthy canyoneering objectives than the more celebrated defiles of Zion, the Escalante, Canyonlands, or the almighty Grand Canyon itself, it is first necessary to understand what is and what isn't properly termed canyoneering in the eyes of Mr. Fisher, who is something of a zealot when it comes to this newly christened phylum of backcountry play. True canyoneering, according to him, is a hybrid of rock climbing, river running, and bust-ass backpacking; if what you're doing doesn't involve a healthy slice of all three, it's simply not the genuine article.

Fisher's enthusiasm about canyoneering on the Mogollon Rim is owed to the complex makeup of the escarpment's underlying geology, that being a thoroughly scrambled pudding of igneous, metamorphic, and sedimentary rock. The jumbled arrangement of hard and soft strata creates a canyon architecture that not only varies tremendously from drainage to drainage, but tends to be embellished with multi-tiered cascades, fiendish water boxes, and wickedly narrow slots. "Other places in the world have bigger and more extensive canyons than the Mogollon Rim," Fisher declares, "but nowhere are the canyons more special, and hardly anywhere are they more challenging."

Fisher likes challenge as much as the next guy, but he is especially

△ 107

fond of the imposing design of the Mogollon canyons, because it helps keep out fraternity boys, gun nuts, ordinary duffers, and other riffraff. "I probably know a couple of hundred guys who do slot canyons like the Escalante, Buckskin-Pariah, Zion Narrows. They're pretty spectacular places, but for the most part they demand nothing more than some tough hiking to get to. As a consequence, a place like Zion Narrows might get twenty people parading through it on a nice spring day. Whereas the narrows of West Clear Creek, which is the best known of the Mogollon canyons, probably doesn't see more than four or five parties in an entire year. Heck, there are four big canyons in northwestern Arizona— I'm not going to tell you which ones—that haven't yet had a single documented descent."

The sparse traffic means that most of the environmental and cultural treasures of the Mogollon country remain remarkably unsullied. Fisher pointed out two canyons within eighty miles of metropolitan Phoenix that still shelter unexcavated cliff dwellings. He confessed, "I could probably make a pretty good living raiding cliff dwellings for Mogollon pots—people sell them for big money on the black market—but I couldn't live with myself. Among the canyoneers I know, there's a very very strong ethic about not disturbing anything in the cliff dwellings. One of my buddies found a beautiful pot, perfectly intact, buried up to its neck in the sand. He dug it up to have a look, then reburied it again—just up to its neck, exactly like he'd found it—and continued on his way."

Rick Fisher can fairly lay claim to being the world's leading authority on the Mogollon canyons and the myriad secrets they contain, having explored more of them than any person alive, but it wasn't until the late 1970s that he first visited one. He made his initial foray while a student at the University of Arizona after hearing rumors of a strange and wondrous place called the White Pools, supposedly tucked somewhere in the upper reaches of West

Clear Creek—a tributary of the Verde River that flows off the Rim thirty miles southeast of Sedona.

It took him a full day of bushwhacking through crumbling cliff bands and a sea of catclaw thorns just to descend from the rim to the canyon floor. That night he was awakened by something rustling around inside his pack; when he turned on his flashlight to investigate he was greeted by a coiled blacktail rattler staring him in the face. Moving up the creek the next morning, the walls of the canyon narrowed to a vertical-walled slot; at one point three large logs were jammed between these walls sixty feet overhead, sobering testimony to the force and height of the waters that surge down the canyon during flash floods.

A mile into the narrows, Fisher encountered the first in a series of what he calls "water boxes"—pools that are too deep to wade and impossible to climb around—forcing Fisher and his two companions to swim. The difficulty of swimming with a fully loaded backpack, not to mention keeping its contents dry, eventually convinced Fisher to start carrying a tiny inflatable raft—small enough to fit easily inside a pack, but buoyant enough to float a week's food and gear in front of a swimmer—on subsequent canyoneering efforts. Such mini rafts were soon widely recognized as essential pieces of canyoneering gear, but not before the chairman of the Phoenix chapter of the Sierra Club drowned in 1979 while attempting to make it through the West Clear Creek narrows without one.

For all the trials of Fisher's first Mogollon trip, the experience turned him into a canyoneering fanatic: He has been back to West Clear Creek more than ten times. He has also gone about methodically bagging most of the other Mogollon canyons, constantly refining his tools and techniques along the way. "One thing I learned pretty quick," Fisher says, "is that every Mogollon canyon is different. And a slight difference in the geologic makeup of a canyon can make a huge difference in the gear you'll need, the techniques

△ 109

required, the best season to attempt a particular descent. What works in West Clear Creek won't necessarily work in Salome, what works in Salome won't work at all in Tonto; a beautiful place in May can be deadly in July."

Fisher also learned how to divine the location of the most interesting canyons—which according to the prevailing canyoneering aesthetic are those with the narrowest slots, the most photogenic waterfalls, the deepest, clearest pools—from telltale contours on a U.S.G.S. quadrangle. "To find a good canyon on a map," he says, "first you look for a peak high enough—which means about eight thousand feet in this region—to catch the rain. Then you analyze the size of the catchment basin above the canyon you're interested in: It generally has to cover at least ten miles by twenty miles to result in a stream with enough flow to cut a decent canyon. Next, you examine the closeness of the contour lines: They have to indicate a formation that's both deep and very narrow; you can have a really really deep canyon, but if it's too wide there won't be anything interesting in it."

"Finally," Fisher continues, "you check out the geology. If the geologic makeup isn't exactly right, most of the stream's water will sink into the ground, even in a large drainage system, and you won't wind up with any pools or waterfalls, which are what I go into canyons to find." By weighing all these factors collectively, he maintains, you can usually determine whether any given canyon is worth a visit.

But not always. For a number of years Fisher had noted a chasm on the map—he calls it Crystal Canyon rather than its real name to keep its location secret—that looked fairly promising in every regard except its geologic makeup, which was uniformly igneous. "That," he says, "usually results in a pretty boring canyon, so I gave up on it. Turned out I was wrong. Like *way* wrong." One day a pilot who knew of Fisher's obsession with canyons told him that he'd happened over Crystal and noticed "some really big waterfalls." Fisher immediately decided to hang the geology and go have a look.

Getting into the canyon involved hiking across a plateau that was crawling with a particularly aggressive race of black diamondback rattlesnakes ("they were only three or four feet long," Fisher relates, "but thick as a muscular arm, and with these real broad, evil-looking heads") and then scrambling down to the creek bottom over two hundred feet of vertical rimrock. Some Mogollon petroglyphs eventually led the way to a route through the basalt cliff bands, but, Fisher insists, "it was serious climbing all the same. Those Mogollon dudes were pretty fair climbers, and they sure weren't afraid of heights."

The risks Fisher took, however, paid handsome dividends. Not only did the waterfalls prove to be all Fisher hoped they'd be, "but there were cliff dwellings in the canyon, and some of the deepest, clearest pools in all of Arizona. And the walls above one of these pools were studded with millions of quartz crystals, some in huge clusters. They weren't gem quality, but they were incredible all the same. So, you can understand why I've tried to keep this canyon a secret. You can go in there any day of the year—I've been back six times—and I guarantee you'll never see another soul."

Obsession is a funny thing. One can only speculate what quirks of upbringing or chromosomal architecture cause some people to go overboard on Rotisserie League baseball, while others become Shriners or dedicate their lives to growing the perfect tomato; who's to say why Rick Fisher has wrapped his life so tightly around the canyons of the desert Southwest?

For the better part of a decade Fisher has been visiting the Mogollon canyons at every opportunity, for work and for play, documenting their otherworldy forms in thousands of photographs, testifying before Congress to protect them with official Wilderness status. He has used the canyons' considerable charms to successfully

△ 111

romance more than a few women, unsuccessfully rehabilitate scores of juvenile delinquents, and introduce a like number of handicapped children and assorted city slickers to the pleasures of the back-country.

Paradoxically, however, to the extent that Fisher is known at all in the world at large, it is not for his association with the canyons of the Mogollon Rim, but for his deeds in the barrancas of the Mexican Sierra Madre, about which he has written a popular guide book, and where, for the past several years, he has derived the bulk of his livelihood working the adventure travel racket.

It was in the Sierra Madre, in 1986, that Fisher pulled off his most noteworthy canyoneering accomplishments to date: descents of two of the deeper canyons in North America, the Sinforosa and the Urique. The latter was the site of Fisher's closest canyoneering scrape to date, and it had nothing to do with Class VI white water or radical rock climbing.

Fisher took two companions on the Barranca de Urique trip, a woman named Kerry Kruger and her boyfriend, Rick Brunton. The three had paddled and portaged a small rubber raft down the canyon for three days without incident when they passed from the state of Chihuahua into Sinaloa, a district notorious for its marijuana and heroin cultivation. That night they pulled off the river to camp at the confluence of a small side creek, and Fisher set out on foot to search for some clear drinking water. Almost immediately, he blundered into a cornfield that looked unusually green; when he looked more closely he saw that each cornstalk supported a young pot plant. "I walked quickly back to the boat," Fisher remembers, "and said, 'Guys we've got to load up and get out of here quick.'"

Fisher explains that the campesinos in that part of Mexico "can't begin to understand why rich gringos would take the trouble to float down their remote river unless they were spies for the DEA, hunting for drugs. We paddled like hell for an hour to avoid a confrontation, but the river went around in a big meander, so all our paddling brought us right back by the pot field. We came around a bend, and both sides of this narrow river were lined with scraggly looking men armed with rifles, squatting down on their heels. One guy was standing; he was dressed in a nice shirt and a nice cowboy hat and carried an automatic pistol instead of a rifle. He called out to us to come over, saying he wanted to buy some cigarettes. We replied, 'We don't smoke, it's bad for your lungs.' For some reason they all thought that was pretty damn funny."

Fisher ultimately defused the situation by showing the big cheese with the pistol a folder of press clips he always brings along just for such incidents. Convinced Fisher was anything but a DEA agent, the pot growers allowed the boaters to continue on their way. A short while later they came to a village. According to Fisher, "There were no roads within 150 miles of the place: it looked like something out of a Clint Eastwood flick, with horses tied up to hitching posts and all these Mexicans walking around with scars on their faces and rifles slung over their shoulders, looking at us like we'd just climbed off a space ship."

Before they pushed on, Fisher went into the center of town to take some photographs of a crumbling eighteenth-century mission while Kruger and Brunton kept an eye on the boat. While Fisher was away, three drunk young men who had been toasting the profitable delivery of a large load of pot to the village airstrip came down to the water and started hassling the gringos for amusement. As Fisher was walking back down to the boat, one of the Mexicans tried to kiss Kruger, prompting Brunton to step between them; Fisher arrived on the scene just in time to see the Mexican poke the muzzle of a gun squarely into Brunton's chest.

Once again, Fisher managed to ease the tension before anybody came to harm. This time, amazingly enough, he did it by scolding the gunmen in pidgin Spanish: "Taking care not to establish eye contact—which would have been taken as provocation—I started screaming at them, telling them they were *muy malo hombres*, that they should be ashamed of themselves for bothering innocent tourists. And it worked. The leader gave me a sharp shove on the shoulder, then they put their guns away and left." Shaking uncontrollably, Fisher and company hopped in the boat and paddled away as fast as their arms would propel them.

Canyoneering needn't be so rich in adrenaline, of course, nor does it have to involve travel to distant lands. This was impressed upon me near the end of my week in the Mogollon country with Fisher and his friends, when we visited a canyon the locals call Salome Jug. As the buzzard flies, it's not fifty miles from the canyon to the Scottsdale city limits—at night the lights of Phoenix glow on the western horizon like a movie marquee—but Salome was the most alluring of the five Mogollon canyons I spent time in. If a trip down some grueling chasm like Tonto Creek or the Barranca de Sinforosa is the canyoneering equivalent of going on a major mountaineering expedition in the Himalaya, traveling through Salome Jug is analogous to climbing a sunny three-pitch route in the Shawangunks.

A half-hour stroll down an abandoned jeep road lined with flame-tipped ocotillo and thousands of towering saguaro brought us to the rim of the defile. It was narrow enough to spit across, and dropped in a clean two-hundred-foot drop to the sparkling waters of Salome Creek. A rappel looked inevitable until Fisher guided us to a hidden system of natural ramps, down which we scurried with ease to the canyon floor.

Salome Jug ran for just half a mile from end to end, but what it lacked in scope was more than made up for by the intimacy and intensity of its wildness. The canyon was an utterly spellbinding slice of earth, like no place I had ever seen: The creek burbled by in a chain of long, skinny pools—tinted an astonishing shade of emerald by dissolved minerals—linked by a series of cascades ranging in height from mere inches to more than seventy feet; above this tableau shot walls of rose-colored granite sculpted into striking curves and sensuous angles, and polished smooth as a bowling ball.

We decided to make a game out of making our way from one

end of the Jug to the other, and spent the day stroking across the pools and clambering through the spray of the waterfalls. Whenever the spirit moved us, we stopped to sit in the sun and watch the clouds slide across the cobalt stripe of sky framed by the rim above. Lying on a delicious slab of granite toward evening, letting the warmth of the pink rock suck the chill from my dripping back, it dawned on me that it was my birthday. I couldn't have picked a better place to spend it, I decided, if I'd tried.

9. A MOUNTAIN HIGHER THAN EVEREST?

ON A HOT AFTERNOON IN 1852, LEGEND HAS IT, THE SURVEYOR General of the Great Trigonometrical Survey of India, Sir Andrew Waugh, was sitting in his office in Dehra Dun when a computer named Hennessey (computers in those days being made of flesh and bone rather than disk drives and silicon chips) rushed in and blurted out, "Sir! I have discovered the highest mountain in the world!" The mountain he had "discovered" jutted out of the crest of the Himalaya in the forbidden kingdom of Nepal, and at the time was known only by the Roman number XV. By Hennessey's reckoning it stood a whopping 29,002 feet above mean sea level.

Using precision theodolites, surveyors had repeatedly "shot" Peak XV from the northern plains of India in 1849 and 1850, but until Hennessey got around to computing their data two years later, nobody had the slightest suspicion that Peak XV was unusually high. The surveyors' observation stations were more than a hundred miles from the mountain, and from that distance all but the summit nub of Peak XV is hidden by towering massifs in the foreground, many of which give the illusion of being much greater in stature.

In 1865, when Hennessey's computations had been thoroughly checked and Waugh was convinced beyond a shadow of a doubt that no other mountain in the Himalaya could rival XV in height, he officially christened the peak Mt. Everest, in honor of Sir George Everest, his precedessor as Surveyor General, unaware that the Tibetans who lived to the north of the great mountain already had several names for it that were not only more apt but considerably

▲ 116

more mellifluous, foremost among them *Chomolungma*, which trans-
lates as "Goddess Mother of the Land."

Before Mt. Everest—nee XV, nee Chomolungma—was measured, the title of World's Highest Mountain had been at various
times bestowed upon a number of different peaks. In the seven-
teenth and eighteenth centuries, the prevailing wisdom held that
Chimborazo, a 20,702-foot volcano in the Andes of South America,
was the highest. In 1809 a Himalayan peak called Dhaulagiri was
estimated by a British surveyor to be 26,862 feet high (Dhaulagiri's
height has lately been adjusted to 26,795 feet), and thus had a more
legitimate claim to the title. But most geographers beyond the borders of India thought such an extreme elevation preposterous and
continued to favor Chimborazo until the 1840s, when the title was
transferred briefly to Kangchenjunga, a 28,168-foot neighbor of
Mt. Everest, and finally, in the 1850s, to Everest itself.

Needless to say, once the pinnacle of Mt. Everest had been firmly
established as the highest point on the surface of the earth, it wasn't
long before men decided that Everest needed to be climbed: Getting
to the top, declared G. O. Dyrenfurth, an influential chronicler of
early Himalayan mountaineering, is "a matter of universal human
endeavor, a cause from which there is no withdrawal, whatever
losses it may demand." Those losses, as it turned out, would not
be insignificant: Following Hennessey's momentous announcement
in Sir Andrew's office, it would take the lives of fifteen men, the
efforts of thirteen expeditions, and the passage of 101 years before
the summit of Everest would finally be won.

It wasn't until the early hours of May 29, 1953 that a rangy New
Zealander named Ed Hillary and his compact Sherpa partner,
Tenzing Norgay, found themselves inching up the final airy un-
dulations of the south ridge of Mt. Everest. By late morning, Hillary
later recorded, "we were starting to tire. I had been cutting steps
continuously for almost two hours and wondered, rather dully,
whether we would have enough strength left to get through. I cut

△ 117

around the back of another hump and saw that the ridge ahead dropped away and that we could see far into Tibet. I looked up and there above us was a rounded snow cone. A few whacks of the ice-axe, a few cautious steps, and Tensing [sic] and I were on top." And thus did Hillary and Tenzing, just before noon, become the first men to stand on the summit of Mt. Everest.

Four days later, the morning of Queen Elizabeth's coronation, word of the ascent reached England. "*The Times*," wrote Jan Morris, the journalist who first broke the story (though at the time she was still a he and wrote under the byline "James Morris"), "had printed the news in that morning's editions, the vast Coronation crowds waiting in London's rain had been told in the dark of the night, the world was rejoicing with us; all was well." The conquest of the "Third Pole" (the North and South poles being the first and second) touched off a ground swell of British pride. Hillary was summarily knighted; Tenzing became a national hero throughout India, Nepal, and Tibet (all of which claimed him as one of their own). Every almanac and encyclopedia would record forever thereafter that the first men to conquer the world's mightiest peak were Sir Edmund P. Hillary and Tenzing Norgay. Or so it seemed, at least until March 7, 1987, when a brief story, buried in the back of the *New York Times*, appeared under the headline, "New Data Show Everest May Take Second Place."

The data in question had been gathered in the summer of 1986 by an American expedition to K2—a steep pyramid of brown rock and shining ice that straddles the Sino-Pakistani border some eight hundred miles northwest of Everest. After measuring electromagnetic signals broadcast from a military satellite, a sixty-five-year-old astronomer from the University of Washington named George Wallerstein calculated that K2—long thought to be 28,250 feet high—may actually have an elevation of 29,064 feet, and possibly even as great as 29,228 feet. If Wallerstein's findings proved correct, K2—not Everest, which in 1975 was pegged at 29,029.24 feet by a fastidious Chinese survey—was in fact this planet's highest chunk of terra firma.

In the nearly fifty years since Hillary and Tenzing first paved the way, more than two hundred men and women have struggled to the top of Mt. Everest, and thousands of others have tried and failed, all of which has involved the expenditure of untold millions of dollars, amputations of dozens of frostbitten toes, and the loss, at last count, of more than a hundred human lives. All those who made these sacrifices were firm in the belief that in doing so they were pursuing the biggest trophy in mountaineering. But if Wallerstein was right, says Lance Owens, the leader of the 1986 American expedition to K2, "it means that everybody's been climbing the wrong mountain." Indeed, if Wallerstein was right, honors for making the premiere ascent of the world's tallest peak would belong not to Hillary and Tenzing, but to a pair of little-known Italian climbers named Lino Lacedelli and Achille Compagnoni, who, in 1954, became the first men to stand on top of K2.

Most expert geographers and geodecists, however, were quick to warn that it was a little early for Hillary to hand in his knighthood or for Italians to start popping champagne corks; Wallerstein himself repeatedly made clear that his "observations were of a preliminary nature," and that it would be a mistake to declare that K2 is definitely higher than Everest until both mountains could be meticulously resurveyed with modern satellite technology. Wallerstein was well aware that recent Himalayan history does not lack for instances in which men have claimed to have discovered the existence of one mountain or another that surpassed Everest in elevation, only to be proven woefully wrong upon close inspection of their evidence.

In the early 1930s, for instance, there was a flurry of excitement over an impressive-looking peak called Minya Konka (now known as Gongga Shan) that towers over a remote corner of China's Sichuan province. In 1929, after returning from an expedition across that part of the world in search of the giant panda, Kermit and Theodore Roosevelt, Jr., sons of the rough-riding president, wrote a book in which they alluded to claims that Minya Konka "rises more than 30,000 feet and is the highest in the world." Adding credence to these rumors were the reports of one Joseph Rock, a self-taught botanist with a flair for the dramatic and a loose way with the facts. Rock had visited a monastery at the base of Minya Konka, used a pocket compass and a barometer to come up with an estimate for the mountain's height, and then promptly cabled the National Geographic Society: "MINYA KONKA HIGHEST PEAK ON GLOBE 30,250 FEET. ROCK."

The Society, which was sponsoring Rock's explorations in China, balked at publishing that figure, and subsequent, less sloppy, surveys would show Minya Konka to be but 24,900 feet high, nearly a mile beneath Everest's summit. No matter, though, for Rock had hedged his bet by reporting that another peak, four hundred miles north of Minya Konka, was also at least 30,000 feet high. This peak, believed to be the dwelling place of gods by the fierce aboriginal people who lived at its foot, was called Anye Machin (now Magen Gangri), and rumors of its great altitude would persist long after those about Minya Konka had been laid to rest.

The seeds of the legend of Anye Machin were planted by Brigadier General George Pereira, an accomplished British explorer who in 1921 embarked from Beijing upon an ambitious journey, intending to trek through Tibet, India, Burma, and southern China before returning to Beijing. Pereira died en route, but in 1923, before expiring, he bumped into Rock in the Chinese province of Yunnan and told him of an immense peak in the Anye Machin Range that he was sure would prove higher than Everest. Rock immediately resolved to go there.

Rock made the arduous trip to Anye Machin in 1929, and estimated its height from a distance of about sixty miles—once again using nothing more than what Galen Rowell, the photojournalist/mountaineer who in 1981 made one of the first ascents of Anye

Machin, has described as "compass sightings, altitudes calculated from the boiling point of water, and his usual zeal to come up with an astounding figure." Mr. Rock determined that the elevation of Anye Machin was 29,529 feet, some 500 feet higher than Everest.

The speculation about Anye Machin's height lay dormant for most of the next two decades. It flared up again in a big way, however, near the end of World War II, thanks to a story that appeared in a score of international newspapers. In 1944, an American DC-3 participating in the airlift from Burma over the "Hump" to Chunking was reportedly blown far off course by a violent storm. Somewhere in the vicinity of the Anye Machin Range the pilot climbed out of a layer of clouds at 30,500 feet—the plane's altimeter, the pilot said, was working perfectly—and looked up to see a snow-covered peak jutting far above the cloud ceiling, hundreds of feet higher than his aircraft.

That famous flight, as it happens, was fabricated wholesale (a DC-3 can't fly anywhere near 30,500 feet) by bored Twentieth Air Force officers looking to play a joke on British war correspondents who had been pestering the pilots for gripping stories of derring-do. In 1947, however, when a fifty-five-year-old American pen manufacturer named Milton "Ball-Point" Reynolds first read about that "flight" in a new book by James Ramsey Ullman, he—like most of the rest of the world—hadn't been apprised of the hoax. What Reynolds did know was that Ullman, in *Kingdom of Adventure: Everest* had concluded a passage about Anye Machin thus: " . . .if the mystery mountain is indeed higher than Everest, its discovery will rank as the most important geographical event of modern times."

Reynolds—a short, round, balding millionaire with a penchant for publicity—liked to bill himself as the inventor of the ballpoint pen. In fact, the ballpoint was the brainchild of a Hungarian named Laszlo Biro; Reynolds just brought it to the American public. Claiming of his newfangled instrument that, among other attributes, "It Writes Under Water!" (neglecting to add that in truth

△ 121

the pen was often barely functional on perfectly dry paper), Reynolds managed to sell $13 million worth of pens within a year.

In April 1947, accompanied by a crackerjack twenty-seven-year-old test pilot named Bill Odom, Reynolds had broken Howard Hughes's around-the-world flying record. No sooner had the considerable hubbub from that stunt subsided than Reynolds was struck with an idea for bettering it: He and Odom would fly to China and prove that Anye Machin was the 30,000-plus-foot mountain spied by the Burma airlift pilots.

Reynolds and Odom embarked for China on February 29, 1948, in a giant four-engine C-87 christened the *China Explorer*, which had been specially outfitted with state-of-the-art aerial surveying instruments. In Reynold's entourage was the renowned alpinist and mountain surveyor Bradford Washburn, recruited from Boston's Museum of Science to ensure that Anye Machin would be accurately measured. In the plane's cargo hold were ten thousand gold-plated ballpoint pens that were to be a gift for Madame Chiang Kai-shek. When one of Reynolds's assistants pointed out that the balls in the gold pens were malfunctioning, that they didn't write worth a damn, Reynolds replied, "I know, but the Chinese can't write anyway, and they'll be glad to have them."

The expedition did not get off to a good start. In Beijing, while taxiing to the runway prior to taking off for Anye Machin, Odom got the C-87 stuck in the mud, and then attempted to free the plane by gunning the engines. As the Chinese and American scientists on board peered out the windows in horror, the right landing gear collapsed from the strain and the big plane dropped to its belly, rupturing a fuel tank and destroying one of the propellors. Nobody was injured, but Reynolds sadly announced that the expedition was over.

By and by the landing gear was repaired, and Reynolds and Odom flew the C-87 to Shanghai to get a new propellor that they hoped would enable them to get the expensive aircraft back to the United States. After the propellor was replaced, though, Reynolds was struck by an inspiration: He proposed to Odom that instead of heading home, they make an unannounced (and highly illegal) flight directly from Shanghai to Anye Machin without Washburn or any meddling Chinese observers, measure its height themselves, and then proceed directly to Calcutta.

They took off with this scheme in mind on April 2, but Odom underestimated the fuel they would need to pull it off. Anye Machin was fifteen hundred miles from Shanghai, Calcutta was another two thousand miles beyond that, and by the time the China Explorer neared the mountain Odom realized they would have to turn around immediately if they were to avoid a crash landing somewhere in the wilds of Tibet. "At that instant," Reynolds later wrote, "I saw ahead a huge mass of land coming out of the strata of clouds below and reaching right up into the 31,000-foot overcast . . . At last, I was actually looking at the highest mountain in the world!"

The *China Explorer* made it back to Shanghai with fifteen minutes worth of fuel left in its tanks, whereupon the Chinese, who were boiling mad, promptly impounded the aircraft and escorted the Americans to their hotel under armed guard. Reynolds was unrepentant. A few days later he and Odom sneaked back to their plane to attempt an escape. As Reynolds told it, no sooner had they gotten inside the aircraft than an angry "mob of Chinese" approached. As a diversionary tactic, Reynolds hurled his last two hundred gold pens out the door at them, Odom gunned the engines while the Chinese fought among themselves for the pens, and the Americans skimmed away under a hail of bullets.

Reynolds and the *China Explorer* made it back to America safe and sound, but without much in the way of proof that Anye Machin was higher than Mt. Everest. To rectify that, in 1949 an explorer named Leonard Clark traveled to the base of Anye Machin with a crude theodolite borrowed from a Chinese highway bureau and measured the peak to be 29,661 feet high. "I believe without question," he insisted upon his return, "that I have found the highest mountain in the world."

△ 123

Citing the deaths of General Pereira in 1923 and Bill Odom in a plane crash at a Cleveland air show in 1949, Clark also insisted that Anye Machin was "jinxed" by a curse that had brought misfortune to "every explorer, flyer, and adventurer after even briefly sighting this so-called god mountain." A few years later Clark disappeared without a trace while exploring a South American jungle. Clark's measurement of Anye Machin, sadly, did not fare any better than he did: Careful surveys by the Chinese in the 1970s determined the true elevation of the mountain's highest point to be a humdrum 20,610 feet.

So, was Wallerstein's estimation of K2's height in 1986 as suspect as Clark's and Rock's and Reynolds's erroneous estimations of Anye Machin's height? If not, how could a mountain of such unremarkable proportions as Anye Machin be considered a contender for Mt. Everest's title for the better part of five decades, when, until this year, it occurred to nary a soul that K2—a mountain that stands some eight thousand feet higher than Anye Machin—might also be a contender?

The answer to the first question was maybe—but then again, maybe not. Regarding the second question, it should be explained that, unlike Anye Machin, both Everest and K2 (which was named and first triangulated by the British in 1856, the peak's colorless moniker being a surveyor's designation of convenience that happened to stick) had been expertly surveyed and resurveyed so many times that their order of rank had come to be accepted by virtually everybody as immutable.

Measuring mountains, however, is a fiendishly difficult task, one in which there is ample room for errors to be made. As Louis Baume explains in *Sivalaya*, a compendium of facts about the world's fourteen highest mountains, "The calculation of the heights of Himalayan peaks is a realm of such erudite complexity that not even angels armed with theodolites and plumb-lines would dare to tread therein."

△ 124

To calculate a mountain's elevation the traditional way, by triangulation, a surveyor first uses a theodolite to "shoot" the angle of the peak's rise from at least two different locations, each of which has a known altitude. After measuring the distance between the two theodolite stations, he knows the dimensions of two angles and one side of a huge imaginary triangle delineated by the mountain's summit and the two stations. After plugging these three numbers into a simple trigonometric formula, then correcting the result to compensate for the curvature of the earth, he knows the height of his mountain.

Ignoring, for the moment, the whole question of how the surveyor knows the height of his theodolite stations in the first place, let us consider some of the thornier problems he has to grapple with in the procedure outlined above. In crunching the numbers to arrive at the peak's height, for example, the surveyor must somehow take into consideration such wild cards as atmospheric refraction and plumb-line deflection. The latter, in the simplest terms, is the tendency for the immense mass of a range like the Himalaya to tug the liquid leveling bubbles in a surveyor's instruments slightly toward the mountains—in the same way that the moon tugs on the tides—and thus throw them out of whack.

The former phenomenon, refraction, is the tendency for light rays—the same light rays that create the image of the mountain in the eyepiece of the theodolite—to bend as they pass through the atmosphere between mountain and surveyor, causing the mountain to appear higher than it really is. The precise amount of this warp is a crucial but slippery variable that hinges on such factors as the temperature and density of every atmospheric layer through which the light has passed.

Between sunrise and noon, for instance, as the atmosphere warms up and its refraction properties shift, the triangulated elevation of a distant peak can easily "shrink" several hundred feet. And the effect of this variable on a surveyor's figures swells exponentially with each additional mile between the surveyor and the mountain.

△ 125

In arriving at an elevation for Everest from stations on the far plains of India, surveyors have had to correct their height calculations by as much as 1,375 feet to compensate for estimated refraction.

All of the head-scratching mentioned thus far, however, is just the final piece of the puzzle. If you haven't first correctly assembled the rest of the puzzle—which gives you the height of your final theodolite stations—shooting your mountain will be a waste of time.

The crux of the problem in determining a mountain's height above sea level is figuring out, as Wallerstein describes it, exactly "where the sea would be if it were lapping at the mountain's base instead of a thousand miles away." The survey stations from which Everest's height was triangulated by the British lay more than a thousand miles from the survey's starting point, at the city of Madras on the southeast coast of India; in the case of K2 the survey stations were more than seventeen hundred miles from Madras. Before either mountain could be measured, the altitude of the final survey stations had to be established by a complex chain made up of thousands of independent triangulations carried link by laborious link across the whole of the Indian subcontinent. That sort of work, says David N. Schramm, former head of the department of astronomy and astrophysics at the University of Chicago, "is like building a house of cards. Each level of data is built on the previous one. If one level is off, the deck collapses."

In his 1986 measurement of K2, Professor Wallerstein was able to completely sidestep the elaborate "house of cards," from which all earlier K2 surveyors had made their calculations, by relying on a seventy-five-pound suitcase-size instrument called a Doppler receiver. This particular Doppler receiver was designed to analyze radio waves beamed down by a network of six satellites originally put into orbit by the U.S. Navy as a navigational aid for submarines. By measuring subtle shifts in the "pitch" of these signals as a satellite passes overhead (the same oft-observed Doppler effect that causes the sound of a siren to fall off sharply in pitch when a

△ 126

police car whizzes past) the instrument can determine the latitude, longitude, and altitude of wherever it's been plunked down to a much, much greater degree of accuracy than could ever be determined by even the most careful chain of triangulations from a seacoast: If ten or twelve satellite passes are monitored and averaged out, a Doppler receiver can figure out where on the earth's surface it is to within a spherical meter of its true position.

Accurate though Doppler receivers are, they are also prohibitively expensive (a good one costs upwards of eighty thousand dollars) and in relatively short supply. Since nobody had any reason to suspect that the accepted elevations of Everest and K2 might be way off the mark, the instruments had always been reserved for more demonstrably practical applications—pinpointing mineral reserves, locating downed aircraft—than checking the height of the Himalayan giants. When Wallerstein and Lance Owens came across a used Doppler receiver at a bargain price, however, they decided to take the instrument with them to K2, just for the hell of it.

On June 8, 1986—a clear, crisp day on the Karakoram plateau of southwestern China—Wallerstein erected the antenna of his Doppler receiver on a small knoll at the base of K2, turned it on, and took a fix on his altitude from a satellite speeding by seven hundred miles overhead. Then, by means of that precise base elevation and an ordinary theodolite, Wallerstein triangulated the altitude of several surrounding landmarks that he knew had last been surveyed in 1937 by the British explorer Michael Spender.

Upon returning to Seattle, Wallerstein discovered, much to his surprise, that the elevations Spender had recorded for those landmarks were all about nine hundred feet lower than his. Since Spender had used the summit of K2—which he assumed to be 28,250 feet high—as the sole benchmark from which every other elevation in his survey was derived, Wallerstein concluded that the long-accepted elevation of K2 must also be about nine hundred feet too low: By his calculations, K2 might actually be higher than Everest, maybe by as much as several hundred feet.

Upon arriving at those numbers, Wallerstein—who is a distinguished astronomer and a conscientious scientist, but has little experience as a surveyor—emphasized that, because of the limited nature of his survey, he wasn't saying K2 *was* higher than Everest, only that it *might* be. The primary aim of the expedition Wallerstein joined was to climb K2 (the team got to 26,500 feet on the peak's north face before being defeated by the same storms that contributed to the deaths of thirteen people on the other side of the mountain), not measure it, so Wallerstein was obliged to spend the bulk of his time in China hauling loads of food and climbing gear up the lower reaches of the massif. By the time his load-carrying responsibilities were completed, he only had a few days left to conduct his survey.

Furthermore, the solar battery recharger the expedition had counted on to keep the Doppler receiver powered up failed to work. As a consequence, the machine was able to record just one satellite pass before its batteries were drained. Although the thirty-two separate readings the receiver made from that solitary pass were very clear, without subsequent passes their accuracy could not be confirmed.

Despite these shortcomings, and Wallerstein's own caveats about the speculative nature of his upwardly revised measurement of K2, the news that K2 might well be higher than Everest created quite a stir, especially in Italy. Immediately after *Outside* magazine and The *New York Times* simultaneously broke the story, Wallerstein was deluged with interview requests from Italian newspapers and television stations. In addition to the Italians, most mountaineers around the world (with the possible exception of those who had climbed Everest) were rooting hard for K2, feeling that because it was both a prettier mountain and a much harder one to climb, K2 *deserved* to be higher. Throughout the brouhaha, nevertheless, Bradford Washburn—who had played a key role in bursting Anye Machin's bubble—insisted that when the dust cleared Mt. Everest would still be on top. And if not? "Well," the eminent surveyor allowed, "then I think Ed Hillary might be a little shook up."

Within a week of the publication of Wallerstein's findings, several teams announced plans to settle the matter once and for all by resurveying both K2 and Everest using Doppler technology. The first of these expeditions to come back with the goods, ironically, was an Italian team led by Ardito Desio, the same Ardito Desio who led the Italian expedition that had made the first ascent of K2 back in 1954. After taking meticulous satellite readings beneath both Everest and K2—and ignoring what must have been a strong temptation to fudge the numbers in K2's favor—Desio announced his findings on October 6, 1987: Everest, 29,108 feet; K2, 28,268 feet. Hillary and Tenzing, no doubt, breathed a mighty sigh of relief.

10. THE BURGESS BOYS

Spring has supposedly arrived in the Front Range of Colorado, but the sky hangs low and an icy breeze slices through Eldorado Canyon as Adrian Burgess, a thirty-nine-year-old Englishman living in Boulder, muscles his way up the steep red sandstone of a climb called C'est La Vie. One hundred and thirty feet up, he stops at a sloping ledge, secures the rope to a pair of bolts, and belays his three partners, one by one, up to his stance. The last of these climbers is Adrian's identical twin, Alan.

As Alan arrives at the exposed perch, the wind picks up dramatically and a squall commences to dust the belay ledge with snow. Alan eyes the 5.11 microholds that kick off the next pitch, then levels his gaze at Adrian and says, " 'Bout time for the Bustop to be opening, don't you think, Youth?"

The Bustop is a bar that enjoys a great deal of Alan's business whenever he's in Boulder visiting Adrian in between the Himalayan expeditions that have held sway over the twins' lives for the past nine years. Alan favors the Bustop, he says, because it's just up the street from Adrian's home. It probably doesn't hurt that the Bustop offers two beers for a buck during happy hour, and happens to be a topless joint besides.

After an efficient retreat from the walls of Eldorado, the Burgess entourage rolls stylishly up to the entrance of the Bustop in a rusting slab of Detroit iron—Adrian's greatest material asset—to which a bumper sticker has been affixed that reads "A Fool and His Money are Soon Partying." Inside the bar's cavernous, dimly lit chambers, most of the dancers seem to know Alan; several smile warmly and greet him by name as he leads the way to a table overlooking the runway. Our waitress is a woman named Susan who Alan first met in Periche, a high Sherpa village on the trekking route to Mt. Everest. Probably nowhere but in Boulder, it occurs to me, would one encounter strippers who spend their vacations trekking in Nepal.

When we sit down, Adrian appears ill at ease, "It's Lorna," Alan tells me under his breath. "Aid's not supposed to come in 'ere." Lorna, the well-to-do niece of a United States congressman, is Adrian's wife of seven years. As soon as the opportunity presents itself, Alan surreptitiously slips one of the Bustop's distinctive matchbooks into the pockets of Adrian's coat, on the off chance that Lorna might someday come across it and demand an explanation. "Want to keep the lad on 'is toes," Alan whispers with a wicked grin.

Fortunately, Adrian is a virtuoso at staying on his toes, and so, for that matter, is Alan. But then, when you're allergic to work, you subsist on charm and the occasional petty scam, and when you spend a sizeable chunk of every year dodging death on the roof of the world, you get in plenty of practice.

The Burgess twins occupy a unique niche in modern alpine society. In a subculture that has come to be dominated by clean-living, hard-training, high-profile Frenchmen and Germans and Austrians who pose for Alfa Romeo ads and lend their names to lines of chic clothing, the twins remain low-lying pub-crawlers and brawlers, forever staying just one step ahead of the authorities. They are among the last of a breed of working-class British climbers for whom how much one drinks and with whom one fights have always been as important as what mountains one climbs. Although their names mean absolutely nothing to most of the world, within that small, ingrown, multinational fraternity obsessed with finding harder and harder ways up higher and higher mountains, the Burgess boys are luminaries of the brightest magnitude.

Rail thin and tall, with perennially pale skin, long English faces, and dirty blonde Prince Valiant coifs, Adrian and Alan Burgess wouldn't look at all out of place playing rhythm guitar in a mid-sixties British rock band—the Animals, maybe, or The Who. The twins were born and raised in the working-class village of Holm-firth, at the edge of the vast Yorkshire moors—the same empty, brooding tracts that gave birth to the novels of the Brontë sisters. In the case of the Burgess brothers, their childhood rambles across the moors brought them in contact with rough-and-tumble northern English climbers. These older climbers filled the twins' impressionable young heads with tales of the bold deeds and outrageous acts of Don Whillans, Joe Brown, and other hard-drinking gritstone heroes, irrevocably fixing the course of the Burgess's lives.

The twins took up climbing at the age of fourteen, and immediately began to pursue the sport with a vengeance. At seventeen they went to the Alps for the first time, and were shortly polishing off many of the most fearsome routes in Chamonix and the Dolomites; they had heard their British elders spinning yarns about legendary climbs like Les Droites and the Freney Pillar, and assumed that getting up big-name nordwands by the skin of one's teeth was the norm on the Continent. When they were twenty-four, in 1973, they expanded their alpine horizons by driving overland to India in a beat-up mini van, where they pushed a difficult new route up an 18,000-foot Himalayan peak called Ali Rattna Tibba.

During the early seventies, the Yorkshire lads worked off and on in England's burgeoning outdoor education racket, conducting Outward-Bound-style courses for juvenile delinquents. "They were what you Americans call 'oods in the woods programs," Adrian explains, "only in our case it was 'oods leading the 'oods in the woods."

The twins moved to Canada in the midseventies, where they landed construction jobs in Calgary by presenting themselves as highly skilled carpenters, when in truth all they knew about building was what they had hastily gleaned from a library book the night before applying for work. It was also in Canada that Alan obtained landed immigrant status, with the attendant rights and benefits, by claiming to be an ace VW mechanic, the skills of which no one else in the city apparently possessed. Work, however, even in the outdoors, proved to be a lot less fun than climbing, so the Burgesses decided it was something they could do without. Aside from a few momentary lapses, the twins proudly point out, neither has held an honest job since 1975.

That was the year they began to wander the globe in earnest, pubbing and brawling in the finest Whillans tradition. They were arrested in four countries, and reprimanded in many more. In Lima, Peru, they precipitated a slug-fest in a bordello after accusing the establishment of false advertising. In Talkeetna, Alaska, the locals are still peeved about the time the Burgesses and six British cronies absconded with thirty cases of beer from the Fairview bar and narrowly escaped going to jail.

In the course of their travels, the twins also bagged route after harrowing route, from Fitzroy to McKinley, Huascaran to the Howser Towers, Les Droites to Logan to the Grandes Jorasses. "Our lives pretty much turned into one long run of trips," Al reflects with an air of incredulity. "There've been so many that it's sometimes 'ard to tell 'em apart."

The Burgess's string of ascents did not go unnoticed in the British climbing community. As early as 1975, in fact, Chris Bonington considered inviting them on his historic expedition to the southwest face of Everest—a route hyped as "the hardest way up the highest mountain in the world." The expedition eventually put Dougal Haston and Doug Scott on the summit, but the twins' names never made it onto the team, most likely, Alan speculates, "because we'd some'ow developed a reputation for occasionally getting a bit disorderly, and Bonington, very much a media man, didn't want anybody along who might blow 'is cool for 'im."

When the twins realized that their "reputation for occasionally getting a bit disorderly" might preclude their ever being invited on

△ 133

an expedition to a major Himalayan peak, they decided to take matters into their own hands. In 1979 they joined forces with a friend named Paul Moores and went to Nepal to attempt an audacious alpine-style ascent of 26,041-foot Annapurna II. They were turned back by hurricane-force winds at 23,500 feet, but that taste of rarefied Himalayan air only whetted their appetites for more of it; the Burgesses have returned to the Himalaya or Karakoram every single year since.

Last fall it was Lhotse—Mt. Everest's nearest neighbor, the fourth-highest mountain in the world—that received the twins' attention. Nineteen eighty-seven, as it turned out, was not a good year to climb in the Himalaya. Storms ripped through the range with such frequency and violence that not a single climber made it to the top of either K2 or Everest, the first time in sixteen years that the summit of the latter was not attained. The twins were understandably relieved, therefore, halfway up Lhotse, when September 27 dawned bright and promising over the Khumbu region of Nepal.

Alan was breaking trail high on Lhotse's southeast buttress, followed on the rope by Adrian and an acquaintance from Colorado named Dick Jackson. The great amount of fresh snow on the peak made the party think twice about avalanche conditions, but the slope felt reassuringly solid beneath the knee-deep mantle of powder; with a dozen Himalayan expeditions under his belt, Alan figured he could tell when a hill was safe and when it wasn't. Furthermore, it seemed important to make the most of the fair weather in a season that had seen so little of it.

At 23,000 feet, the route up Lhotse zigged and zagged through a series of ice cliffs. Alan was leading past one of these seracs over easy ground, casually belayed from below by his brother, when his hypoxic reveries were cut short by a deep, muffled _WOOOMPF_! Alan looked up to see the jagged gash of a fracture line rip across the slope and calve off an immense slab of wind-packed snow, five feet thick and one hundred fifty feet across, directly above his stance.

For an instant, the slab seemed to move in slow motion, but as it tore free from the last of its fragile underpinnings and committed itself to the valley, a vertical mile below, the mass of snow began to accelerate with alarming speed. After traveling forty feet, the leading edge of the slab slammed squarely into Alan's chest. "I tried to scramble on top of it," he remembers, "but there was no bloody way. I went under, and then there was blackness, and all I could think was, 'Shit, so this is what it feels like to die.'

"But after maybe three seconds," Alan continues, "I suddenly popped back up to the surface, facing downslope, up to me waist in the avalanche, with all this 'eavy snow pulling at me legs. Instinctively, I threw me 'ead back, went into a full arch, and the whole thing slide underneath me."

It was, however, a case of having jumped out of the frying pan into the fire: The avalanche had by that time engulfed his two ropemates, and was rapidly carrying them toward the lip of a two-hundred-foot ice cliff. Alan had just enough time to plant his ice axe and dig in his heels before the rope to Adrian and Jackson jerked tight at his waist, threatening to yank him off the side of Lhotse once again.

With the weight of his partners stretching the rope tight as piano wire, and Alan's tenuous attachment to terra firma about to fail, his impromptu belay pulled Jackson and Adrian up to the surface of the snow slide, allowing the avalanche to pass beneath them. When Alan finally arrested their tumble, Jackson and Adrian were only ten feet from the edge of the cliff.

The following afternoon, recovering at base camp, they noticed a lammergeier—a species of Tibetan vulture with a nine-foot wingspan—circling in the updrafts overhead. This was puzzling, for lammergeiers were never seen unless there was a dead yak or other carrion in the vicinity, and there was no reason for any yaks to be near. The puzzle was solved a day later, when the twins accompanied the doctor from a Spanish expedition to the toe of the mountain to search for four overdue teammates, and came upon bits and pieces of climbing gear scattered across a large avalanche fan.

The missing Spaniards had been attempting to climb Lhotse by a route adjacent to the one taken by the Burgesses and Jackson and had been caught in a similar avalanche on the very same morning. The Spanish climbers, though, hadn't been so lucky: All four of them were swept six thousand feet to their deaths. A thorough search of the run-out zone turned up the mangled remains of two of the bodies, which Alan and Adrian helped the doctor bury. "Man," Adrian recalls with a shudder, "that was a 'orrible job." It was not, however, a job the twins were unaccustomed to.

Any alpinist who sets his sights on the higher reaches of the Himalaya stands a fair chance of being party to someone's premature demise; for those who attempt 8,000-meter peaks with the frequency of the Burgess brothers, it is a statistical inevitability. They had both been present in 1982—Alan as a member of a massive Canadian Everest expedition; Adrian with a small New Zealand team attempting Lhotse from the west—when first an avalanche in the notorious Khumbu Icefall, and then a collapsing serac, killed five of their cohorts. The twins had also been on K2 that ugly summer in 1986 when the mountain took the lives of no less than thirteen men and women, including the leader of their expedition, the acclaimed English climber Alan Rouse, whose companions (not the twins) had been forced to abandon him, comatose but still alive, in a tent at 26,000 feet to save their own skins.

By Adrian's reckoning, more than half of the twins' climbing colleagues have, as he put it, "gotten the chop," the majority of them in the Himalaya. But if the implications of this gruesome tally bothers the Burgess boys, it doesn't show. Dealing with risk, walking the fine line, playing a game of ever-escalating brinkmanship—this is what the cutting edge of climbing has always been

△ 136

about. Those who elect to participate in this hazardous pastime do so not in spite of the unforgiving stakes, but precisely because of them.

Even after the unpleasant business with the dead Spaniards underscored the closeness of their shave with the avalanche last September, the twins gave no thought to abandoning their original plan to climb the southeast buttress of Lhotse, traverse its long, spectacularly serrated summit ridge, descend the distant west side of the peak, and then, for a finale, run the gauntlet of the Khumbu Icefall to reach the base of the mountain. Alan actually managed to convince himself that their brush with death had bettered their odds—from then on, they'd be more cautious.

A week after the avalanches, the twins, Dick Jackson, and another Coloradan, Joe Frank, went back up on the peak, only to be stopped at 21,700 feet by even worse avalanche conditions than before. The twins still weren't ready to give up on the mountain, however. They decided that the route that had killed the Spaniards looked safer than their own, so Alan departed for the village of Namche Bazar to get their climbing permit changed to the Spanish line.

"While Al was down in Namche," says Adrian, "this mega storm 'it the 'imalaya, the biggest of the 'ole bloody year. Dumped more than four feet of snow in thirty-six hours." During the second night of the storm, Adrian was lying in his tent at base camp when the back side of the sturdy dome suddenly collapsed, smashed flat under a mass of snow. Unable to get to the door, he cut his way out to discover that a small avalanche—just a slough, really—had slid noiselessly off the hillside above camp, crushed half his shelter, and stopped a foot short of burying him. His brother's tent, a few yards away, was completely buried beneath six feet of cement-like avalanche debris. "If Al 'ad been in it that night," Adrian gravely postulates, "there's no question what the outcome would've been."

The next morning, Adrian set out for Namche to find Alan. The walk out required breaking trail through chest-deep snow; it took two hours to make the first mile, a distance he'd normally cover in

△ 137

fifteen minutes. After another mile, beneath Island Peak, Adrian came upon the base camp of a Royal Air Force expedition. "It looked like it'd been 'it by a fuckin' bomb," he says: "'alf the tents were flat, two bodies were lying nearby, all that showed of another body was this frozen 'and sticking out of the snow. The survivors said a fourth body was still buried somewhere, they didn't know where, and that a Tamang porter 'ad gone crazy after the avalanche, thrown off all 'is clothes, and run off into the night. All I could think was, 'Oh man, is this shit really 'appening?' "

The naked porter was eventually found, frostbitten and hypothermic, but alive. Adrian hoisted him onto his back with a tumpline and lit out for Chhukun, the nearest settlement, seven miles distant. Halfway there, Alan appeared, coming up the trail. "Eh up, youth," Adrian greeted him, "good to see you. Give this fucker a ride, will you?" The brothers ran the rest of the way down to Chhukun together, taking turns carrying the porter, and managed to reach the village in time to save his life.

The Burgesses were finally forced to give up their Lhotse expedition. But before they'd even arrived back in Kathmandu, they were hatching schemes to raise funds for a K2 expedition the following summer; one of these schemes involved convincing *The National Enquirer* that Alan Rouse might still be alive after spending two years in a tent at 26,000 feet (nobody had been back to the upper reaches of K2 since Rouse had been abandoned in August, 1986). The twins would return with the story of how he had survived by cannibalizing his fallen comrades, and in return ask the *Enquirer* for a modest honorarium—say, ten or twenty thousand dollars.

As it happened, the *Enquirer* deal never got off the ground, but the twins managed to get to the Karakoram regardless. At the end of May they set up a base camp at the foot of K2; as this is being written—if all has gone according to plan—the Burgess boys should be arriving at the summit.

* * *

Then again, they might not be. In scanning their climbing record, one is struck by how often success in the Himalaya has eluded the Burgesses: The twins have tried and failed to climb Annapurna II, Nanga Parbat, Ama Dablam, Everest (twice for Alan, once for Adrian), Lhotse (three times for Adrian, twice for Alan), Cho Oyu (twice for Alan), and K2; the only major Himalayan peaks they've actually seen the summits of, in fact, are 24,688-foot Annapurna IV and 26,795-foot Dhaulagiri. If climbers kept track of batting averages, Adrian would be hitting about .200 in the Himalayan Leagues, Alan a lowly .167.

These unimpressive numbers can be attributed at least in part to the twins' habit of going after very tough routes with very small teams, and on many occasions intentionally making those routes tougher still by attempting the climbs in the screaming winds and unimaginable cold of the Himalayan winter. Paradoxically, the twins chalk up the scarcity of big summits in their lives to a "cautious nature." Alan insists that "among our peer group in England, we've always 'ad a reputation for being careful climbers, for not sticking our necks out that much. Why is why we're still alive, I suppose, and most of them are not."

While both twins concede that dumb luck has a lot to do with who survives and who doesn't in the Himalaya, they also argue that the great majority of mountaineering accidents are preventable. "We look at it," says Adrian, "that most tragedies 'appen because climbers make mistakes. Sure, we're capable of making mistakes, too, but if you keep your eyes open, and don't climb for the wrong reasons, you won't make as many of them."

Alan says the deaths of two of their closest friends, Al Rouse and Roger Marshall (who, in 1985, fell while trying to solo the North Face of Everest) are perfect examples of what can happen when people climb for the wrong reasons. "Both Roger and Rouse," Alan explains, "died because they were pushing to meet outside pressure. Rouse's situation back in England was such a mess—the woman 'e loved 'ad left him, and a woman 'e didn't love was about to 'ave 'is baby—that going back 'ome without 'aving summited was something 'e just couldn't face. In Roger's case, 'e was under incredible financial pressure to get up Everest; 'e needed to summit so 'e could write a successful book and pay off some loans that were 'anging over 'is 'ead and keeping 'im tied to the wife and family 'e was trying to get free of. It's 'ard enough making the right decisions at 'igh altitude without having that kind of pressure clouding your judgment."

If caution and mountain sense have contributed to the twins' failures, their critics—of whom there are many—are quick to cite other, less charitable, reasons for the frequency of their washouts. Even the Burgess boys' most vocal detractors grudgingly admit that the twins are exceptionally strong at high altitude—that they seem, in fact, to perform as well as any climber alive in the cold, meager air found at those extreme heights known as the "Death Zone." But Gordon Smith—an erstwhile Burgess pal from Calgary who accompanied the twins to Annapurna IV, Everest, and Manaslu— maintains that the lads' freewheeling, "What, me worry?" modus operandi just doesn't cut it on 8,000-meter peaks. "There's a lot more to getting up a big mountain than being able to put one foot in front of the other," Smith states matter-of-factly, "and the twins haven't a clue how to organize an expedition. Somehow, something goes wrong on every one of their Himalayan trips."

On the Manaslu expedition, according to Smith, the twins' stubbornness led to critical shortages of important gear, such as snow pickets. On the same expedition, a group of trekkers who'd paid hefty fees for the privilege of accompanying the climbers to the first camp were, upon reaching the mountain, arbitrarily denied the opportunity when Alan became impatient with the novices. Smith feels the twins' shortcomings as expedition leaders stem in part from their trying to do too much. "It's very difficult," he explains, "to be up at the front all day, pushing the route hard, and then have enough energy at night to properly oversee the expedition logistics."

But Smith disapproves of more than the twins' managerial skills. "They know how to be charming when it suits them," he continues bitterly, "but basically they're just a couple of con artists. They don't seem to care how many enemies they make; when they get caught out they just change their friends and move on to a fresh set of marks." If Smith's disaffection with the twins seems rather pointed, it might have something to do with the fact that their last trip together—the unsuccessful attempt on Manaslu in 1983—concluded with a disagreement over Alan's handling of expedition finances that escalated into a no-holds-barred fistfight in the streets of Kathmandu.

Spend any time in Chamonix, or Llanberis, or the chang houses of the Khumbu, and you'll come to appreciate that there is no shortage of stories about the Burgess boys, their quick fists, and their brazen scams. "Wherever you go in Nepal," says American climber/physician Geoffrey Tabin, "as soon as the local people see that you're a Westerner, they excitedly ask you 'You know Burgess? You know Burgess?' The guys are living legends on four continents; Alan's sexual escapades alone could fill several volumes of 'Penthouse Letters.' "

One of the more recent additions to the wealth of Burgess lore originated amid the weirdness and bright lights of Las Vegas, at the annual outdoor trade show. The twins were in attendance, putting the touch on industry bigwigs for funding and free gear for their Lhotse expedition. After a hard day of hustling, the twins made the rounds of the usual parties, where Alan met a friendly native who invited him to have a nightcap in her hotel room.

Alan, Adrian, and Alan's newfound friend were driving down the Strip in Adrian's beater truck, en route to Adrian's hotel, when a low-slung car, carrying several Vegas cowboys, pulled alongside at a red light. Adrian, to make small talk, held up the beverage he'd been sipping and yelled out the window, "This American beer tastes like piss!" in his best Yorkshire accent.

At the next red light, the low-slung car again pulled alongside the twins' truck, and two of the cowboys jumped out. Adrian also jumped out and, being a firm believer in the preemptive strike, immediately punched one of the cowboys. Because Adrian was so drunk, however, he lost his balance while completing the round-house and fell on his face before the cowboy could return the punch. Alan, seeing his brother on the pavement and assuming he'd been coldcocked, jumped out and bloodied the hapless cowboy's nose (the second cowboy had by this time scurried back to the security of the low-slung car). Alan then collected Adrian, got back in the truck, and roared off down the Strip.

When they stopped for the next red light, the low-slung car pulled directly in front of the twins in a menacing fashion, but none of the cowboys got out. This so angered Adrian that he hopped out of the truck, ran up the back of the low-slung car, and leapt up and down on its roof until the light turned green and the car peeled away.

Unfortunately for the cowboys, though, the traffic lights just weren't turning for them that evening: the next one in their path was also red. Alan pulled the truck up behind the low-slung car, paused for a moment, and then rammed it smartly. Then he put the truck in reverse, backed up a few feet, and rammed the car again.

By now the cowboys realized that they'd made a grave error in judgment in tangling with the Burgesses. The cowboys decided To hell with the red light, punched the car's accelerator, and promptly slammed into an oncoming vehicle. Alan, disappointed that the fun with the cowboys had come to an end, steered around the twisted metal and broken glass, and motored slowly on down the Strip toward Adrian's hotel.

Shortly thereafter, five police cars surrounded the truck with lights flashing and sirens wailing, and Alan was yanked out of the

△ 142

cab and spread-eagled across the hood. The cops said they wanted to ask Alan a few questions about an alleged assault on some local citizens, followed by a hit-and-run accident. Alan politely explained that the cops had it all wrong, that he and his equally innocent brother, who were in town on important international business, were the victims, not the perpetrators, of the assault. And as for the accident, Alan said, the thugs who attacked them had simply collided with another car while trying to flee the scene of the crime.

As Alan continued to embellish upon this theme, the cops warmed up to the story. It had the ring of truth, they thought. They liked Alan. They liked his respectful, Boy Scout attitude, and his comical accent, which they mistook for Australian. Alan, in fact, reminded the cops a lot of this guy in a movie they'd just seen, this Crocodile Dundee fellow.

From that point on, the cops were putty in the Yorkshireman's hand. Great movie, that Crocodile Dundee, the cops told him, Alan ought to check it out. The cops went on to say how genuinely sorry they were that Alan had been attacked in their usually peaceful city, and they hoped he didn't judge all Americans by the behavior of a few bad apples. And then they wished him a friendly good night.

Of all the preposterous twists and turns in the Burgess saga, perhaps none is more preposterous than the pairing of Adrian and Lorna Rogers. Adrian, after all, is by his own admission a destitute, uncultured thirty-nine-year-old adolescent, while Lorna is as upper crust as they come. Her family has been at the summit of Denver society for four generations; theirs is a world of polo ponies and coming-out parties and very exclusive country clubs, a world where one's children are expected to go to the right schools and marry into the right families. Lorna—an intense, strong-willed, very attractive attorney—did the debutante routine in all its splendor, went to college at Williams, has a sitting congressman, Mo Udall, for an uncle, and likes to unwind by riding thoroughbreds in fox

△ 143

hunts. And in 1981, eleven months after meeting him in Kathmandu's Yak and Yeti bar, she married Adrian Burgess, bad boy of the Himalaya.

When I asked Lorna what she thought of having a husband who was absent four or five months of every year, she admitted she'd been "really miserable for the first couple of years, but now I kind of like it; I like the pattern of coming and going, the way it keeps the relationship from getting stale. I get to have a husband and share a life with him, but I also get to have a lot of freedom. Actually, Adrian being gone isn't nearly as bad as the way these goddamn expeditions monopolize the household when he's getting ready to go."

Adrian has spruced up his act some under Lorna's considerable influence. The renowned honky-tonker and street-fighter, for instance, has lately taken to riding in the family fox hunts, decked out in full regalia. Whillans is no doubt spinning in his grave, but according to Adrian, "It gets a bit exciting, if you want to know the truth. Riding those 'orses is like sitting on a fast motorbike that goes where it wants to, not where you steer it."

There are not yet any fox hunts on the other twin's horizon. Alan remains the consummate lowballer, a grand master of the art of getting by, living proof of Eric Beck's oft-quoted dictum, "At either end of the socioeconomic spectrum there lies a leisure class." Alan, observes his ex-friend Gordon Smith, "has no visible means of support; he never seems to do any work, yet somehow he always scrapes by. It's a bit of a mystery how he manages it, really."

One way he manages it is to spend most of his time, even between expeditions, living in Nepal with Sherpa friends. "I suppose I average about six or seven months a year over there," Alan says. "It's a lot cheaper to stay in Nepal between trips, living on three dollars a day, than to fly back to the West. Of course, to get by on that you 'ave to be willing to eat the same things the Sherpas eat, and eating potatoes and lentils and kurd three times a day can get a bit boring. And that kind of money won't allow you to drink beer, you 'ave to stick to chang and rakshi.

"I don't mind dirt-bagging it, though. I've actually come to prefer the Third World lifestyle," Alan continues. "When I come back to the West now, I become confused by all the choices. You really feel the culture shock, the difference between a culture that 'as some depth and one that only thinks it 'as. My gut's grown accustomed to the Sherpa flora, right, so I never get sick over there anymore, but as soon as I come back 'ere—like to Vancouver or somewhere?—BANG! I get the shits, the congested chest, the 'ole bloody business."

By living in high Sherpa villages, Alan is also able to sneak off and climb illicitly, without the hassle of permits, peak fees, or liaison officers. In the winter of 1986, for instance, he and a Sherpa friend ducked into Tibet with their Sherpani girlfriends and managed to come within a day of summiting on an 8,000-meter peak. "It was all 'ighly illegal, of course," Alan says, "but it was the biggest adventure I've 'ad in the last eight years; it was great. We went super light: just one tent, two mats, and two sleeping bags for the four of us. During the trek over to the mountains, we 'ad to listen carefully for yak bells, and lie low whenever Tibetan traders came up the trail, because they'll sell you out to the Nepalese check posts if they see you."

Over the eight years Alan has intermittently lived and climbed in the Khumbu district of Nepal, he has developed a remarkable rapport with the Sherpa people. Because few Western climbers can come close to matching the performance of Sherpas in the Himalaya, most Sherpas privately condescend to sahibs. "They tend to regard Westerners as chumps," Alan states flatly. Because Alan is unusually strong at altitude for a white boy, and has learned, like a Sherpa, to carry monstrous loads with a tump-line around his forehead, he has earned a rare degree of Sherpa respect. "In some ways," Alan brags, "they consider me a local."

△ 145

That consideration is at least partly due to the fact that in June, 1987, a twenty-one-year-old Sherpani named Nima Diki gave birth to Alan's son in a bed of leaves at thirteen thousand feet in the village of Phortse. Alan allows, "When I got the letter from a Sherpa friend warning me, 'Nima Diki's looking a little big,' I thought, 'Oh fuck, what am I going to do?' But when I got over there and saw the little guy, I stopped worrying."

It remains to be seen whether the arrival of the child, named Dawa, will finally bring Alan's protracted adolescence to a close—as he prepares to enter his fifth decade—and actually usher him into the world of adult responsibility. He has, however, been overheard mulling over such adult-sounding dilemmas as whether or not Dawa should go to school in Kathmandu or in the Khumbu.

Meanwhile, Chris Bonington—apparently no longer concerned about the twins' reputation—recently invited Adrian and Alan on a major expedition, scheduled for the spring of 1989, to attempt the only significant unclimbed line remaining on Mt. Everest: the notorious northeast ridge, where Britain's two finest Himalayan climbers, Joe Tasker and Peter Boardman, disappeared back in 1982. Because the 1989 expedition will be a typical Bonington extravaganza—involving sixteen western climbers, thirty Sherpas, live television broadcasts, siege tactics, bottled oxygen—and both Adrian and Alan have had unpleasant experiences on big-budget, big-team Himalayan efforts, the twins respectfully declined the invitation.

After participating in Alan Rouse's large and ill-fated expedition to K2 in 1986, says Adrian, "We decided, absolutely, that from then on we would climb only with each other, and never again with a huge team." Owing to the expedition's complex logistics, the Burgesses were almost never ropemates on K2, and were profoundly unhappy because of it.

Sherpas believe that identical twins—*zongly*, they call them—are imbued with exceptional luck. Lucky or not, the power of the bond between twins cannot be overestimated. Their relationship has a built-in intimacy that at times seems almost clairvoyant. "With your twin," Adrian says, "you always know just what 'e's thinking, just what 'e's going to do. There's this tremendous trust: you couldn't lie to your twin, even if you wanted to; 'e'd see right through it straight away. On a big trip, on the other 'and, because of all the expedition politics you're never in total control of your own climbing. Somebody at base camp decides who you should climb with, when you should go up, when you should go down. And that's dangerous."

Adrian speculates that Bonington's upcoming Everest expedition is likely to be particularly hazardous in that regard. "Because of all the money being spent," he explains, "and the direct involvement of the media, the climb is going to be hyped-up like crazy. And the climbers will start believing all that hype, of course, and develop a 'go-for-it' mentality. Personally, I think somebody's going to get killed."

That somebody, notes Adrian, could all too easily be a Burgess were they to go along. "I've learned to accept death as a part of life in the mountains," Adrian reflects. "I've even learned to accept it when close friends die. But I don't think I could handle it if Al died; I couldn't accept that."

It's likely that pride, as well as caution, played a part in the twins' decision not to join Bonington. On the huge 1982 Everest expedition, by all accounts, Alan Burgess did more to make the climb a success—in terms of route preparation, leadership, and load carrying—than any other member of the team, yet poor timing and a malfunctioning oxygen mask denied him the opportunity to stand on the summit. That, in itself, might not have bothered Alan un-duly had he not seen the post-expedition glory—and financial spoils—go almost exclusively to those who summited.

According to Gordon Smith, who also did more than his share of the work on Everest but did not summit, "When we left base camp after the climb, all eight climbers still felt very friendly to-wards each other. Then we arrived in Kathmandu, and the media started separating us into winners and losers. The guys who got to the top, the winners, received all the recognition—and quite a bit of money as well, from endorsement contracts and the like. The rest of us went back home to find that we had no jobs, no money, no reward. You find yourself thinking, Jesus Christ, I did a lot more work on that mountain than the bloke who happened to summit; is there any fairness in that?"

So, the question of whether the twins would be going to Everest in 1989 was an open-and-shut case, or at least seemed to be. A few days after Alan left for K2, however, I received a postcard from him. He'd experienced a change of heart, he said, and decided that he was going to accompany Bonington to Everest after all, even though Adrian remained adamant about not going. Since I'd recently listened to both brothers hold forth at a table in the Bustop about the evils of mega-expeditions in general, and this Everest expedition in particular, I phoned Adrian—who had not yet departed for K2—to get the lowdown.

"Al's always been a good rationalizer," Adrian offered, "and now 'e's telling 'imself that the route's a lot more difficult than 'e first thought, and therefore warrants the use of oxygen and fixed rope and a massive team and all that other crap. I think the real reason 'e's all of a sudden decided to go is that, basically, going to Everest means three free meals a day and a place to call 'ome for three months." A long, uncharacteristic silence followed. Finally, Adrian said, "Well, that's me brother, isn't it?"

11. A BAD SUMMER ON K2

IN THE NORTHERNMOST CORNER OF PAKISTAN, IN THE HEART OF THE Karakoram Range, is a forty-mile tongue of rubble covered ice called the Baltoro Glacier, above which rise six of the seventeen highest mountains on the planet. In June, 1986, there were 150 tents pitched at the head of the Baltoro, sheltering expeditions from ten nations. Most of the men and women living in those tents, whose ranks included some of the world's most ambitious and highly regarded climbers, had their sights set on a single summit: K2.

At 28,250 feet, the summit of K2 is some 800 feet lower than Mt. Everest, but its sharper, more graceful proportions make it a more striking mountain—and a much harder one to climb. Indeed, of the fourteen mountains in the world higher than eight thousand meters, K2 has the highest failure rate. By 1985 only nine of the twenty-six expeditions that had attempted the peak had succeeded, putting a total of thirty-nine people on the summit —at a cost of twelve lives. In 1986 the government of Pakistan granted an unprecedented number of climbing permits for K2, and by the end of the summer an additional twenty-seven climbers had made it to the top. But for every two people who summited, one would die—thirteen deaths in all, more than doubling the number of fatalities in the preceding eighty-four years. The toll would raise some thorny questions about the recent course of Himalayan climbing, a course some people believe has become unjustifiably reckless.

AUTHOR'S NOTE: The original version of this piece, published in *Outside* Magazine, was co-written with Greg Child.

The new modus operandi leaves so little margin for error that climbers now commonly begin their ascents with the understanding that if things go wrong, the bond between ropemates—a bond that was until recently held to be sacrosanct—may be discarded in favor of a policy of every man for himself.

The present direction of high-altitude mountaineering was set, it is generally agreed, in the summer of 1975, when Reinhold Messner and Peter Habeler pioneered a new route up a 26,470-foot neighbor of K2's called Hidden Peak without bottled oxygen, a support team, fixed ropes, a chain of preestablished camps, or any of the other siege tactics that had traditionally been de rigueur in the Himalaya. Messner pointedly termed this bold new approach "climbing by fair means," implying that it was cheating to get to the top of a mountain by any other way.

In a single stroke, Messner and Habeler significantly upped the ante in a game that did not lack for high stakes and long odds to begin with. When Messner first announced that he would climb an 8,000-meter Himalayan peak in the same manner that climbers tackled routes in the Tetons and Alps, most of the world's foremost climbers labeled the plan impossible and suicidal. After Messner and Habeler succeeded, anyone with designs on usurping Messner's throne—and more than a few of the men and women camped beneath K2 in 1986 had such designs—was left with little choice but to attack the highest mountains in the world by equally "fair" and incautious means.

The most coveted prize on K2 was its striking South Pillar, huge and unclimbed, a "last great problem" that Messner had nicknamed "the Magic Line." Soaring two vertical miles from glacier to summit, it demanded more steep, technical climbing at extreme altitude than anything previously done in the Himalaya.

There were four teams attempting the Magic Line in 1986, including an American party under the leadership of a thirty-five-year-old Oregonian named John Smolich. Early on June 21, a bright, cloudless morning, Smolich and partner Alan Pennington were climbing an easy approach gully at the base of the route when, far above them, the sun loosened a truck-size rock from the ice, sending it careering down the mountainside. As soon as the boulder struck the top of the gully, a fifteen-foot-deep fracture line shot across the low-angled snowfield, initiating a massive avalanche that engulfed Smolich and Pennington in a matter of seconds. Climbers who witnessed the slide quickly located and dug out Pennington, but not quickly enough to save his life. Smolich's body, buried under thousands of tons of frozen debris, was never found.

The surviving members of the American team called off their climb and went home, but the other expeditions on the mountain regarded the tragedy as a freak accident—simply a matter of being at the wrong place at the wrong time—and continued their own efforts without pause.

Indeed, on June 23, two Basques—Mari Abrego and Josema Casimaro—and four members of a French-Polish expedition—Maurice and Liliane Barrard, Wanda Rutkiewicz, and Michel Parmentier—reached the summit of K2 via the mountain's easiest route, the Abruzzi Spur. Liliane Barrard and Rutkiewicz thereby became the first women to stand on top of K2, and, more impressive still, they did so without using bottled oxygen.

All six climbers, however, were forced by darkness to bivouac high on the exposed side of the summit pyramid, and by morning the clear, cold skies that had prevailed for the previous week had given way to an intense storm. During the ensuing descent, the Barrards—both very experienced Himalayan climbers with other 8,000-meter summits under their belts—dropped behind and never reappeared. Parmentier guessed they had fallen or been swept away by an avalanche, but he nonetheless stopped to wait for them in a high camp on the off chance that they might show up, while Rutkiewicz and the Basques, whose noses and fingertips had begun to turn black from frostbite, continued down.

That night—June 24—the storm worsened. Waking to a complete whiteout and horrible winds, Parmentier radioed base camp by walkie-talkie that he was descending; but with the fixed ropes and all traces of his companions' footprints buried by fresh snow, he soon became lost on the broad, featureless south shoulder of K2. He staggered around in the blizzard at 26,000 feet with no idea where to go, muttering "grande vide, grande vide" (huge emptiness), as climbers in base camp tried to guide him down over the radio by their recollections of the route.

"I could hear the desperation and fatigue in his voice as he went back and forth in the storm, looking for some clue to the descent," says Alan Burgess, a member of a British expedition. "Finally Parmentier found a dome of ice with a urine stain on it, and we remembered it. By this insignificant landmark we could guide him down the rest of the route by voice. He was very lucky."

On July 5, four Italians, a Czech, two Swiss, and a Frenchman, Benoit Chamoux, reached the summit via the Abruzzi route. Chamoux's ascent was done in a single twenty-four-hour push from base camp, an extraordinary athletic feat, especially considering that just two weeks before, the Frenchman had sprinted up the neighboring slopes of 26,400-foot Broad Peak, top to bottom, in seventeen hours.

Even more extraordinary, though, were the deeds underway on K2's south face: a two-mile-high expanse of steep, ice-plastered rock, avalanche gullies, and tenuously hanging glaciers delineated on one side by the Abruzzi Spur and on the other by the Magic Line. On July 4, the Poles, Jerzy Kukuczka, thirty-eight, and Tadeusz Piotrowski, forty-six, started up the center of this unclimbed wall in light, impeccably pure style, bent on pushing the limits of Himalayan climbing to a whole new plane.

Kukuczka was the heir apparent to Messner's unofficial title as the world's greatest high-altitude alpinist. When he arrived at the base of K2, Kukuczka was nipping at Messner's heels in the race to climb all fourteen 8,000-meter peaks; he had already bagged ten of them, an accomplishment that was especially impressive considering the expense of mounting Himalayan expeditions and the pathetic rate of exchange for Polish *zlotys*. To fund their expeditions, Kukuczka and his Polish comrades had been routinely forced to smuggle vodka, rugs, running shoes, and other unlikely commodities that could be bartered for hard currency.

Just before sunset on July 8, after a lot of extreme technical climbing and four brutal bivouacs (the last two of which were without tent, sleeping bags, food, or water), Kukuczka and Piotrowski struggled to the summit of K2 in a howling storm. They immediately began to descend the Abruzzi Spur. Two days later, totally strung out and still battling their way down through the blizzard unroped, Piotrowski—who, because of numb fingers, had been unable to properly tighten his crampon straps that morning —stepped on a patch of steel-hard ice and lost a crampon. He stumbled, righted himself, then lost the other crampon. An attempt to self-arrest wrenched his ice axe out of his hands, and he was soon hurtling down the steepening slope out of control. Kukuczka could do nothing but watch as his partner bounced off some rocks, then disappeared into the mists.

By now the summer's death toll was beginning to give pause to most of the climbers still on the mountain, but for many the lure of the summit proved stronger. Kukuczka himself departed immediately for Nepal to attempt his twelfth 8,000-meter peak and gain ground on Messner in the race to knock off all fourteen. (The effort would prove to be in vain when Messner reached the summits of Makalu and Lhotse the following autumn, to claim the fourteen-summit crown.)

Shortly after Kukuczka returned to base camp to tell his troubling tale, the thirty-eight-year-old Italian solo climber Renatto Casarotto set out on his third attempt that summer to climb the Magic Line alone. This attempt, he had promised his wife, Goretta, would be his last. Solo ascents of difficult new routes on Fitzroy, Mt. McKinley, and other major peaks in South America and the Alps had given Casarotto a heroic, damn-the-torpedoes reputation, but the Italian was in fact a very cautious, very calculating climber. On July 16, a thousand feet below the summit and not liking the look of the weather, he prudently abandoned his attempt and descended the entire South Pillar to the glacier at its base.

As Casarotto made his way across the final stretch of glacier before base camp, climbers watching through binoculars from the camp saw him pause in front of a narrow crevasse that blocked his path and prepare to hop across it. To their horror, as he did so the soft snow at the edge of the crevasse gave way and Casarotto suddenly disappeared, plunging 130 feet into the bowels of the glacier. Alive but badly injured in a pool of ice water at the bottom of the crevasse, he pulled his walkie-talkie out of his pack and called Goretta. At base camp, she heard her husband's voice whispering over the radio, "Goretta, I have fallen. I am dying. Please send help. Quickly!"

A multinational rescue party immediately set out, reaching the crevasse in the last light of the day. A pulley system was soon rigged, and Casarotto, still conscious, was hauled to the surface of the ice. He stood upright, took a few steps, then lay down on his rucksack and died.

The only expedition on K2 to make no effort to conform to Messnerian ethics was a mammoth, nationally sponsored, team from South Korea. Indeed, the Koreans didn't care how they got to the top of K2, just so long as they got someone from their team there, and then got him back down again in one piece. To that end, they employed 450 porters to haul a small mountain of gear and supplies to base camp, and then methodically proceeded to string miles of fixed rope and a chain of well-stocked camps up the Abruzzi Spur.

Late in the day on August 3, in perfect weather, three Koreans reached the summit using bottled oxygen. After starting their descent, they were overtaken by two exhausted Poles and a Czech

△ 154

who, using conventional siege tactics but no oxygen, had just succeeded in making the first ascent of the route on which Casarotto and the two Americans had perished—Messner's coveted Magic Line. As both parties descended together into the night, a famous Polish alpinist named Wojciech Wroz—his attention dulled by hypoxia and fatigue—inadvertently rappeled off the end of a fixed rope in the dark—the seventh casualty of the season. The next day, Muhammed Ali, a Pakistani porter ferrying loads near the base of the mountain, became victim number eight when he was hit by a falling rock.

Most of the Europeans and Americans on the Baltoro that summer had initially disparaged the ponderous, dated methods by which the Koreans made their way up the Abruzzi Spur. But as the season wore on and the mountain prevailed, a number of these climbers quietly abandoned their previously ballyhooed principles and made free use of the ladder of ropes and tents the Koreans had erected on the Abruzzi.

Seven men and women from Poland, Austria, and Britain succumbed to this temptation after their original expeditions packed it in, and decided to loosely join forces on the Abruzzi. As the Koreans prepared to make their final assault, the ad hoc group made its way up the lower flanks of the mountain. Although this multinational "team" ascended at different speeds and were widely scattered over the route, all five men and two women had reached Camp IV at 26,250 feet—the highest camp—the evening before the Koreans mounted their successful summit bid.

While the Koreans made their way to the top in the flawless weather of July 3, the Austro-Anglo-Polish team remained in their tents at Camp IV, having decided to wait a day to make their own push for the summit. The reasons for this decision are not entirely clear; whatever the explanation, by the time the European team finally started up the summit tower on the morning of the fourth, the weather was about to change. "There were great plumes of clouds blowing in from the south over Chogolisa," says Jim Curran, a British climber and filmmaker who was down at base camp at the time. "It became obvious that major bad weather was on the way. Everyone must have been aware that they were taking a great risk by pressing on, but I think when the summit of K2 is within your reach, you might be inclined to take a few more chances than you normally would. It was, in retrospect, a mistake."

Thirty-four-year-old Alan Rouse, one of England's most accomplished climbers, and Dobroslawa Wolf, a thirty-year-old Polish woman, were the first to start up the summit pyramid, but Wolf quickly tired and dropped back. Rouse continued, however, taking on the exhausting work of breaking trail by himself for most of the day until, at three-thirty in the afternoon, just below the top, he was finally caught by Austrians Willi Bauer, forty-four, and Alfred Imitzer, forty. About 4 P.M. the three men reached the summit, and Rouse, the first Englishman to reach the top of K2, commemorated the event by hanging a Union Jack from two oxygen cylinders the Koreans had left. During the threesome's descent, five hundred feet below the summit, they saw Wolf asleep in the snow, and after a heated discussion Rouse persuaded her that she should turn around and go down with him.

Soon thereafter, Rouse also met two other members of the team on their way up, Austrian Kurt Diemberger and Englishwoman Julie Tullis. The fifty-four-year-old Diemberger was a celebrity in western Europe, a legendary _Bergsteiger_ whose career spanned two generations. He had been a partner of the notorious Herman Buhl, and had climbed five 8,000-meter peaks. Tullis, forty-seven, was both a protégée and extremely close friend of Diemberger's, and though she didn't possess a great deal of Himalayan experience, she was very determined, very strong, and had been to the top of Broad Peak with Diemberger in 1984. Climbing K2 together was a dream that had consumed the two of them for years.

Because of the late hour and the rapidly deteriorating weather, Rouse, Bauer, and Imitzer all tried to persuade Diemberger and Tullis to forego the summit and head down. They mulled this advice over, but, as Diemberger later told a British newspaper, "I was convinced it was better to try it finally after all these years. And Julie, too, said, 'Yes, I think we should go on.' There was a risk; but climbing is about justifiable risks." At 7 P.M., when Diemberger and Tullis got to the summit, that risk indeed appeared to have been justified. They hugged each other, and Tullis gushed, "Kurt, our dream is finally fulfilled: K2 is now ours!" They stayed on top about ten minutes, snapped a few pictures, and then, as the gloaming faded into the cold, bitter blackness of the night, turned to go down, joined by fifty feet of rope.

Almost immediately after leaving the summit, Tullis, who was above Diemberger, slipped. "For a fraction of a second," says Diemberger, "I thought I could hold us, but then we both started sliding down the steep slope, which led to a huge ice cliff. I thought, 'My God, this is it. This is the end.' " At the foot of the mountain during the ascent from base camp, they had come across the body of Liliane Barrard, where it had landed following her ten-thousand-foot fall from the upper slopes of the peak three weeks earlier, and the image of Barrard's broken form now flashed into Diemberger's mind. "The same thing," he mused with despair, "is happening to us."

But somehow, miraculously, they managed to stop their slide before shooting over the edge of the ice cliff. Then, fearing another fall in the dark, instead of continuing down they simply hacked out a shallow hollow in the snow and spent the remainder of the night there, above 27,000 feet, shivering together in the open. In the morning the storm was upon them in earnest, Tullis had developed frostbite on her nose and fingers, and she was having problems with her eyesight—possibly indicating the onset of cerebral edema—but the two climbers had survived the night. By noon, when they reached the tents of Camp IV and the company of their five fellow climbers, they thought the worst was behind them.

As the day progressed, the storm worsened, generating prodigious amounts of snow, winds in excess of 100 miles per hour, and subzero temperatures. The tent Diemberger and Tullis were in collapsed under the brunt of the storm, so he crowded into Rouse's and Wolf's tent, and she moved into the tent of Bauer, Imitzer, and Hannes Wieser, an Austrian who hadn't gone to the summit.

Sometime during the night of August 6, while the storm continued to build, the combined effects of the cold, the altitude, and the ordeal of Tullis's fall and forced bivouac caught up to her, and she died. In the morning, when Diemberger learned of her death he was shattered. Later that day, the six survivors used up the last of their food and—even more ominously—the last of their fuel, without which they couldn't melt snow for water.

Over the next three days, as their blood thickened and their strength drained away, Diemberger says they "reached the stage where it is hard to tell dreams from reality." Diemberger, drifting in and out of bizarre hallucinatory episodes, watched Rouse go downhill much faster than the rest of them and eventually sink into a state of constant delirium, apparently paying the price for the energy and fluid he expended breaking trail by himself on the summit day. Rouse, recalls Diemberger, "could speak only of water. But there wasn't any, not even a drop. And the snow that we were trying to eat was so cold and dry that it barely melted in our mouths."

On the morning of August 10, after five days of unabated storm, the temperature dropped to minus-twenty degrees Fahrenheit, and the gale continued to blow as hard as ever, but the snow stopped falling and the sky cleared. Those who were still able to think clearly realized that if they didn't make their move right then, they weren't going to have enough strength left to make a move at all.

Diemberger, Wolf, Imitzer, Bauer, and Wieser immediately started down. They believed they had no chance of getting Rouse down in his semicomatose condition, so they made him as comfortable as they could and left him in his tent. No one harbored any illusions that they would see him again. The five conscious survivors, in fact, were in such bad shape themselves that the descent quickly deteriorated into a case of everyone for himself.

Within a few hundred feet of leaving camp, Wieser and Imitzer collapsed from the effort of struggling through the waist-deep snow. "We tried in vain to stir them," Diemberger says. "Only Alfred reacted at all, weakly. He murmured that he couldn't see anything." Wieser and Imitzer were left where they lay, and with Bauer breaking trail, the other three kept fighting their way down. A few hours later Wolf dropped behind and did not reappear, and the team was down to two.

Bauer and Diemberger made it to Camp III at 24,000 feet, only to find that it had been destroyed by an avalanche. They pressed on toward Camp II, at 21,000 feet, where, after dark, they arrived to find food, fuel, and shelter.

By this time, according to Jim Curran, everyone at base camp had "totally given up hope for the climbers still on the mountain." They were incredulous, therefore, when, as it was getting dark on the following evening, "we saw this figure stumbling slowly down the moraine toward camp, looking like an apparition."

The apparition was Bauer—horribly frostbitten, barely alive, too exhausted and dehydrated to even speak. Eventually he managed to convey that Diemberger, too, was still alive somewhere above, and Curran and two Polish climbers immediately set out to look for him. They found Diemberger at midnight, moving at a crawl down the fixed ropes between Camp II and Camp I and spent all the next day getting him to base camp, from where, on August 16, he and Bauer were evacuated by helicopter to face months in hospitals and multiple amputations of their fingers and toes.

When garbled word of this final disaster reached Europe, it became headline news. Initially, particularly in England, the once-popular Diemberger was vilified by the media for leaving Rouse to die at Camp IV, especially after Rouse, instead of beating a safe and hasty retreat from the high camp on August 5, had waited, apparently, for Diemberger and Tullis to make it down from their overnight ordeal on the summit pyramid.

Curran insists that such criticism is unjustified. Rouse and the others, he believes, stayed at Camp IV on August 5 not primarily to wait for Diemberger and Tullis, but because they "must have been incredibly tired from the day before, and the storm would have made it extremely difficult to find the route from Camp IV to Camp III. The area around Camp IV, remember, is nearly featureless, and everyone was aware that Michel Parmentier had nearly gotten lost trying to find his way down from there in similar conditions."

And when the descent was finally begun from Camp IV, says Curran, "there was absolutely no way that either Diemberger or Willi Bauer could have gotten Rouse off the mountain alive. They were both nearly dead themselves. It was an unimaginably desperate situation; I don't think it's possible to pass judgment about it from afar."

Still, it's difficult to resist the temptation to compare the turn of events in 1986 to a strikingly similar predicament eight K2 climbers found themselves in thirty-three years earlier, at very nearly the same place on the mountain. The climbers, part of an American expedition led by Dr. Charles Houston, were camped at 25,000 feet on the then-unclimbed Abruzzi route, preparing to make a push for the summit, when they were hit by a blizzard of unusual severity that kept them pinned in their tents for nine days. Toward the end of this storm, a young climber named Art Gilkey came down with a deadly ailment called thrombophlebitis, a clotting of the veins brought on by altitude and dehydration.

Gilkey's seven companions, in no great shape themselves, though considerably better off than Diemberger and company, realized that Gilkey stood almost no chance of surviving, and that trying to save him would endanger them all. Nevertheless, says Houston, "So strong had become the bonds between them that none thought of leaving him and saving themselves—it was not to be dreamed of, even though he would probably die of his illness." In the course of being lowered down the mountain, Gilkey was swept to his death by an avalanche, but one can't help but be impressed by how his companions stuck by him to the bitter end, even though in doing so they were all very nearly killed.

It can be argued that the decision not to abandon Gilkey in 1953 was the height of heroism—or that it was a foolishly sentimental act, that had an avalanche not fortuitously taken Gilkey off his teammates' hands, their chivalrous gesture would have resulted in eight deaths instead of one. Viewed in that light, the decision by those who survived K2 in 1986 to leave terminally weakened partners seems not coldhearted or cowardly, but rather eminently sensible.

But if the actions of Diemberger and Bauer appear to be justified, larger, more troubling questions remain. It is natural in any sport to seek ever-greater challenges; what is to be made of a sport in which to do so also means taking ever-greater risks? Should a civilized society continue to condone, much less celebrate, an activity in which there appears to be a growing acceptance of death as a likely outcome?

For as long as people have been climbing in the Himalaya, a significant percentage of them have been dying there as well, but the carnage on K2 in 1986 was something else again. A recent and very comprehensive analysis of the data shows that, from the beginning of Himalayan climbing through 1985, approximately one out of every thirty people who has attempted an 8,000-meter peak has not come back from it alive; on K2 last summer that figure was, alarmingly, almost one out of five.

It is hard not to attribute that worrisome statistic at least in part to Reinhold Messner's remarkable string of Himalayan feats over the past decade and a half. Messner's brilliance has, perhaps, distorted the judgment of some of those who would compete with him; the bold new ground Messner broke may have given unwar-

△ 161

ranted confidence to many climbers who lack the uncanny "mountain sense" that's kept Messner alive all these years. A handful of alpinists from France and Poland may have what it takes to stay at the table in the high-roller's game that Messner launched, but some men and women seem to have lost sight of the fact that the losers in such games tend to lose very big.

Curran cautions that one can't make generalizations about why so many people died in the Karakoram last summer. He points out that "people got killed climbing with fixed ropes and without fixed ropes; people got killed at the top of the mountain and the bottom; old people got killed and young people got killed."

Curran goes on to say, however, that "if anything was common to most of the deaths it was that a lot of people were very ambitious and had a lot to gain by climbing K2—and a lot to lose as well. Casarotto, the Austrians, Al Rouse, the Barrards were all—the word that comes to mind is overambitious. I think if you're going to try alpine-style ascents of 8,000-meter peaks you've got to leave yourself room to fail."

Too many people on K2 that summer, it would appear, did not.

12. THE DEVILS THUMB

By the time I reached the interstate I was having trouble keeping my eyes open. I'd been okay on the twisting two-lane blacktop between Fort Collins and Laramie, but when the Pontiac eased onto the smooth, unswerving pavement of I-80, the soporific hiss of the tires began to gnaw at my wakefulness like ants in a dead tree.

That afternoon, after nine hours of humping 2 × 10s and pounding recalcitrant nails, I'd told my boss I was quitting: "No, not in a couple of weeks, Steve; right now was more like what I had in mind." It took me three more hours to clear my tools and other belongings out of the rust-stained construction trailer that had served as my home in Boulder. I loaded everything into the car, drove up Pearl Street to Tom's Tavern, and downed a ceremonial beer. Then I was gone.

At 1 A.M., thirty miles east of Rawlins, the strain of the day caught up to me. The euphoria that had flowed so freely in the wake of my quick escape gave way to overpowering fatigue; suddenly I felt tired to the bone. The highway stretched straight and empty to the horizon and beyond. Outside the car the night air was cold, and the stark Wyoming plains glowed in the moonlight like Rousseau's painting of the sleeping gypsy. I wanted very badly just then to be that gypsy, conked out on my back beneath the stars. I shut my eyes—just for a second, but it was a second of bliss. It seemed to revive me, if only briefly. The Pontiac, a sturdy behemoth from the Eisenhower years, floated down the road on its long-gone shocks like a raft on an ocean swell. The lights of an oil

▲ 163

rig twinkled reassuringly in the distance. I closed my eyes a second time, and kept them closed a few moments longer. The sensation was sweeter than sex.

A few minutes later I let my eyelids fall again. I'm not sure how long I nodded off this time—it might have been for five seconds, it might have been for thirty—but when I awoke it was to the rude sensation of the Pontiac bucking violently along the dirt shoulder at seventy miles per hour. By all rights, the car should have sailed off into the rabbitbrush and rolled. The rear wheels fishtailed wildly six or seven times, but I eventually managed to guide the unruly machine back onto the pavement without so much as blowing a tire, and let it coast gradually to a stop. I loosened my death grip on the wheel, took several deep breaths to quiet the pounding in my chest, then slipped the shifter back into drive and continued down the highway.

Pulling over to sleep would have been the sensible thing to do, but I was on my way to Alaska to change my life, and patience was a concept well beyond my twenty-three-year-old ken.

Sixteen months earlier I'd graduated from college with little distinction and even less in the way of marketable skills. In the interim an off-again, on-again four-year relationship—the first serious romance of my life—had come to a messy, long-overdue end; nearly a year later, my love life was still zip. To support myself I worked on a house-framing crew, grunting under crippling loads of plywood, counting the minutes until the next coffee break, scratching in vain at the sawdust stuck *in perpetuum* to the sweat on the back of my neck. Somehow, blighting the Colorado landscape with condominiums and tract houses for three-fifty an hour wasn't the sort of career I'd dreamed of as a boy.

Late one evening I was mulling all this over on a barstool at Tom's, picking unhappily at my existential scabs, when an idea came to me, a scheme for righting what was wrong in my life. It was wonderfully uncomplicated, and the more I thought about it, the better the plan sounded. By the bottom of the pitcher its merits

△ 164

seemed unassailable. The plan consisted, in its entirety, of climbing a mountain in Alaska called the Devils Thumb.

The Devils Thumb is a prong of exfoliated diorite that presents an imposing profile from any point of the compass, but especially so from the north: its great north wall, which had never been climbed, rises sheer and clean for six thousand vertical feet from the glacier at its base. Twice the height of Yosemite's El Capitan, the north face of the Thumb is one of the biggest granitic walls on the continent; it may well be one of the biggest in the world. I would go to Alaska, ski across the Stikine Icecap to the Devils Thumb, and make the first ascent of its notorious nordwand. It seemed, midway through the second pitcher, like a particularly good idea to do all of this solo.

Writing these words more than a dozen years later, it's no longer entirely clear just *how* I thought soloing the Devils Thumb would transform my life. It had something to do with the fact that climbing was the first and only thing I'd ever been good at. My reasoning, such as it was, was fueled by the scattershot passions of youth, and a literary diet overly rich in the works of Nietzsche, Kerouac, and John Menlove Edwards—the latter a deeply troubled writer/psychiatrist who, before putting an end to his life with a cyanide capsule in 1958, had been one of the preeminent British rock climbers of the day.

Dr. Edwards regarded climbing as a "psycho-neurotic tendency" rather than sport; he climbed not for fun but to find refuge from the inner torment that characterized his existence. I remember, that spring of 1977, being especially taken by a passage from an Edwards short story titled "Letter From a Man":

> So, as you would imagine, I grew up exuberant in body but with a nervy, craving mind. It was wanting something more, something tangible. It sought for reality intensely, always if it were not there . . .
> But you see at once what I do. I climb.

△ 165

To one enamored of this sort of prose, the Thumb beckoned like a beacon. My belief in the plan became unshakeable. I was dimly aware that I might be getting in over my head, but if I could somehow get to the top of the Devils Thumb, I was convinced, everything that followed would turn out all right. And thus did I push the accelerator a little closer to the floor and, buoyed by the jolt of adrenaline that followed the Pontiac's brush with destruction, speed west into the night.

You can't actually get very close to the Devils Thumb by car. The peak stands in the Boundary Ranges on the Alaska-British Columbia border, not far from the fishing village of Petersburg, a place accessible only by boat or plane. There is regular jet service to Petersburg, but the sum of my liquid assets amounted to the Pontiac and two hundred dollars in cash, not even enough for one-way airfare, so I took the car as far as Gig Harbor, Washington, then hitched a ride on a northbound seine boat that was short on crew. Five days out, when the Ocean Queen pulled into Petersburg to take on fuel and water, I jumped ship, shouldered my backpack, and walked down the dock in a steady Alaskan rain.

Back in Boulder, without exception, every person with whom I'd shared my plans about the Thumb had been blunt and to the point: I'd been smoking too much pot, they said; it was a monu-mentally bad idea. I was grossly overestimating my abilities as a climber, I'd never be able to hack a month completely by myself, I would fall into a crevasse and die.

The residents of Petersburg reacted differently. Being Alaskans, they were accustomed to people with screwball ideas; a sizeable percentage of the state's population, after all, was sitting on half-baked schemes to mine uranium in the Brooks Range, or sell ice-bergs to the Japanese, or market mail-order moose droppings. Most of the Alaskans I met, if they reacted at all, simply asked how much money there was in climbing a mountain like the Devils Thumb.

In any case, one of the appealing things about climbing the

Thumb—and one of the appealing things about the sport of mountain climbing in general—was that it didn't matter a rat's ass what anyone else thought. Getting the scheme off the ground didn't hinge on winning the approval of some personnel director, admissions committee, licensing board, or panel of stern-faced judges; if I felt like taking a shot at some unclimbed alpine wall, all I had to do was get myself to the foot of the mountain and start swinging my ice axes.

Petersburg sits on an island, the Devils Thumb rises from the mainland. To get myself to the foot of the Thumb it was first necessary to cross twenty-five miles of salt water. For most of u day I walked the docks, trying without success to hire a boat to ferry me across Frederick Sound. Then I bumped into Bart and Benjamin.

Bart and Benjamin were ponytailed constituents of a Woodstock Nation tree-planting collective called the Hodads. We struck up a conversation. I mentioned that I, too, had once worked as a tree planter. The Hodads allowed that they had chartered a floatplane to fly them to their camp on the mainland the next morning. "It's your lucky day, kid," Bart told me. "For twenty bucks you can ride over with us. Get you to your fuckin' mountain in style." On May 3, a day and a half after arriving in Petersburg, I stepped off the Hodads' Cessna, waded onto the tidal flats at the head of Thomas Bay, and began the long trudge inland.

The Devils Thumb pokes up out of the Stikine Icecap, an immense, labyrinthine network of glaciers that hugs the crest of the Alaskan panhandle like an octopus, with myriad tentacles that snake down, down to the sea from the craggy uplands along the Canadian frontier. In putting ashore at Thomas Bay I was gambling that one of these frozen arms, the Baird Glacier, would lead me safely to the bottom of the Thumb, thirty miles distant.

An hour of gravel beach led to the tortured blue tongue of the Baird. A logger in Petersburg had suggested I keep an eye out for grizzlies along this stretch of shore. "Them bears over there is just waking up this time of year," he smiled. "Tend to be kinda cantankerous after not eatin' all winter. But you keep your gun handy, you shouldn't have no problem." Problem was, I didn't have a gun. As it turned out, my only encounter with hostile wildlife involved a flock of gulls who dive-bombed my head with Hitchcockian fury. Between the avian assault and my ursine anxiety, it was with no small amount of relief that I turned my back to the beach, donned crampons, and scrambled up onto the glacier's broad, lifeless snout.

After three or four miles I came to the snow line, where I exchanged crampons for skis. Putting the boards on my feet cut fifteen pounds from the awful load on my back and made the going much faster besides. But now that the ice was covered with snow, many of the glacier's crevasses were hidden, making solitary travel extremely dangerous.

In Seattle, anticipating this hazard, I'd stopped at a hardware store and purchased a pair of stout aluminum curtain rods, each ten feet long. Upon reaching the snowline, I lashed the rods together at right angles, then strapped the arrangement to the hip belt on my backpack so the poles extended horizontally over the snow. Staggering slowly up the glacier with my overloaded backpack, bearing the queer tin cross, I felt like some kind of strange *Penitente.* Were I to break through the veneer of snow over a hidden crevasse, though, the curtain rods would—I hoped mightily—span the slot and keep me from dropping into the chilly bowels of the Baird.

The first climbers to venture onto the Stikine Icecap were Bestor Robinson and Fritz Wiessner, the legendary German-American alpinist, who spent a stormy month in the Boundary Ranges in 1937 but failed to reach any major summits. Wiessner returned in 1946 with Donald Brown and Fred Beckey to attempt the Devils Thumb, the nastiest looking peak in the Stikine. On that trip Fritz mangled a knee during a fall on the hike in and limped home in disgust, but Beckey went back that same summer with Bob Craig and Cliff Schmidtke. On August 25, after several aborted tries and some exceedingly hairy climbing on the peak's east ridge, Beckey and company sat on the Thumb's wafer-thin summit tower in a tired, giddy daze. It was far and away the most technical ascent ever done in Alaska, an important milestone in the history of American mountaineering.

In the ensuing decades three other teams also made it to the top of the Thumb, but all steered clear of the big north face. Reading accounts of these expeditions, I had wondered why none of them had approached the peak by what appeared, from the map at least, to be the easiest and most logical route, the Baird. I wondered a little less after coming across an article by Beckey in which the distinguished mountaineer cautioned, "Long, steep icefalls block the route from the Baird Glacier to the icecap near Devils Thumb," but after studying aerial photographs I decided that Beckey was mistaken, that the icefalls weren't so big or so bad. The Baird, I was certain, really was the best way to reach the mountain.

For two days I slogged steadily up the glacier without incident, congratulating myself for discovering such a clever path to the Thumb. On the third day, I arrived beneath the Stikine Icecap proper, where the long arm of the Baird joins the main body of ice. Here, the glacier spills abruptly over the edge of a high plateau, dropping seaward through the gap between two peaks in a phantasmagoria of shattered ice. Seeing the icefall in the flesh left a different impression than the photos had. As I stared at the tumult from a mile away, for the first time since leaving Colorado the thought crossed my mind that maybe this Devils Thumb trip wasn't the best idea I'd ever had.

The icefall was a maze of crevasses and teetering seracs. From afar it brought to mind a bad train wreck, as if scores of ghostly white boxcars had derailed at the lip of the icecap and tumbled down the slope willy-nilly. The closer I got, the more unpleasant it looked. My ten-foot curtain rods seemed a poor defense against crevasses that were forty feet across and two hundred fifty feet deep. Before I could finish figuring out a course through the icefall, the wind came up and snow began to slant hard out of the clouds, stinging my face and reducing visibility to almost nothing.

In my impetuosity, I decided to carry on anyway. For the better part of the day I groped blindly through the labyrinth in the whiteout, retracing my steps from one dead end to another. Time after time I'd think I'd found a way out, only to wind up in a deep blue cul de sac, or stranded atop a detached pillar of ice. My efforts were lent a sense of urgency by the noises emanating underfoot. A madrigal of creaks and sharp reports—the sort of protests a large fir limb makes when it's slowly bent to the breaking point—served as a reminder that it is the nature of glaciers to move, the habit of seracs to topple.

As much as I feared being flattened by a wall of collapsing ice, I was even more afraid of falling into a crevasse, a fear that intensified when I put a foot through a snow bridge over a slot so deep I couldn't see the bottom of it. A little later I broke through another bridge to my waist; the poles kept me out of the hundred-foot hole, but after I extricated myself I was bent double with dry heaves thinking about what it would be like to be lying in a pile at the bottom of the crevasse, waiting for death to come, with nobody even aware of how or where I'd met my end.

Night had nearly fallen by the time I emerged from the top of the serac slope onto the empty, wind-scoured expanse of the high glacial plateau. In shock and chilled to the core, I skied far enough past the icefall to put its rumblings out of earshot, pitched the tent, crawled into my sleeping bag, and shivered myself to a fitful sleep.

Although my plan to climb the Devils Thumb wasn't fully hatched until the spring of 1977, the mountain had been lurking in the recesses of my mind for about fifteen years—since April 12, 1962, to be exact. The occasion was my eighth birthday. When it came time to open birthday presents, my parents announced that they were offering me a choice of gifts: According to my wishes, they would either escort me to the new Seattle World's Fair to ride the Monorail and see the Space Needle, or give me an introductory taste of mountain climbing by taking me up the third highest peak in Oregon, a long-dormant volcano called the South Sister that, on clear days, was visible from my bedroom window. It was a tough call. I thought the matter over at length, then settled on the climb.

To prepare me for the rigors of the ascent, my father handed over a copy of _Mountaineering: The Freedom of the Hills_, the leading how-to manual of the day, a thick tome that weighed only slightly less than a bowling ball. Thenceforth I spent most of my waking hours poring over its pages, memorizing the intricacies of pitoncraft and bolt placement, the shoulder stand and the tension traverse. None of which, as it happened, was of any use on my inaugural ascent, for the South Sister turned out to be a decidedly less than extreme climb that demanded nothing more in the way of technical skill than energetic walking, and was in fact ascended by hundreds of farmers, house pets, and small children every summer.

Which is not to suggest that my parents and I conquered the mighty volcano: From the pages and pages of perilous situations depicted in _Mountaineering: The Freedom of the Hills_, I had concluded that climbing was a life-and-death matter, always. Halfway up the South Sister I suddenly remembered this. In the middle of a twenty-degree snow slope that would be impossible to fall from if you tried, I decided that I was in mortal jeopardy and burst into tears, bringing the ascent to a halt.

Perversely, after the South Sister debacle my interest in climbing only intensified. I resumed my obsessive studies of _Mountaineering_. There was something about the scariness of the activities portrayed in those pages that just wouldn't leave me alone. In addition to the scores of line drawings—most of them cartoons of a little man in a jaunty Tyrolean cap—employed to illustrate arcana like the boot-axe belay and the Bilgeri rescue, the book contained sixteen black-and-white plates of notable peaks in the Pacific Northwest and Alaska. All the photographs were striking, but the one on page 147 was much, much more than that: it made my skin crawl. An aerial

△ 171

photo by glaciologist Maynard Miller, it showed a singularly sinister tower of ice-plastered black rock. There wasn't a place on the entire mountain that looked safe or secure; I couldn't imagine anyone climbing it. At the bottom of the page the mountain was identified as the Devils Thumb.

From the first time I saw it, the picture—a portrait of the Thumb's north wall—held an almost pornographic fascination for me. On hundreds—no, make that thousands—of occasions over the decade and a half that followed I took my copy of *Mountaineering* down from the shelf, opened it to page 147, and quietly stared. How would it feel, I wondered over and over, to be on that thumb-nail-thin summit ridge, worrying over the storm clouds building on the horizon, hunched against the wind and dunning cold, contemplating the horrible drop on either side? How could anyone keep it together? Would I, if I found myself high on the north wall, clinging to that frozen rock, even attempt to keep it together? Or would I simply decide to surrender to the inevitable straight away, and jump?

I had planned on spending between three weeks and a month on the Stikine Icecap. Not relishing the prospect of carrying a four-week load of food, heavy winter camping gear, and a small mountain of climbing hardware all the way up the Baird on my back, before leaving Petersburg I paid a bush pilot a hundred and fifty dollars —the last of my cash—to have six cardboard cartons of supplies dropped from an airplane when I reached the foot of the Thumb. I showed the pilot exactly where, on his map, I intended to be, and told him to give me three days to get there; he promised to fly over and make the drop as soon thereafter as the weather permitted.

On May 6 I set up a base camp on the Icecap just northeast of the Thumb and waited for the airdrop. For the next four days it snowed, nixing any chance for a flight. Too terrified of crevasses to wander far from camp, I occasionally went out for a short ski to kill time, but mostly I lay silently in the tent—the ceiling was

△ 172

too low to sit upright—with my thoughts, fighting a rising chorus of doubts.

As the days passed, I grew increasingly anxious. I had no radio, nor any other means of communicating with the outside world. It had been many years since anyone had visited this part of the Stikine Icecap, and many more would likely pass before anyone did so again. I was nearly out of stove fuel, and down to a single chunk of cheese, my last package of ramen noodles, and half a box of Cocoa Puffs. This, I figured, could sustain me for three or four more days if need be, but then what would I do? It would only take two days to ski back down the Baird to Thomas Bay, but then a week or more might easily pass before a fisherman happened by who could give me a lift back to Petersburg (the Hodads with whom I'd ridden over were camped fifteen miles down the impassable, headland-studded coast, and could be reached only by boat or plane).

When I went to bed on the evening of May 10 it was still snowing and blowing hard. I was going back and forth on whether to head for the coast in the morning or stick it out on the icecap, gambling that the pilot would show before I starved or died of thirst, when, just for a moment, I heard a faint whine, like a mosquito. I tore open the tent door. Most of the clouds had lifted, but there was no airplane in sight. The whine returned, louder this time. Then I saw it: a tiny red-and-white speck, high in the western sky, droning my way.

A few minutes later the plane passed directly overhead. The pilot, however, was unaccustomed to glacier flying and he'd badly misjudged the scale of the terrain. Worried about winding up too low and getting nailed by unexpected turbulence, he flew a good thousand feet above me—believing all the while he was just off the deck—and never saw my tent in the flat evening light. My waving and screaming were to no avail; from that altitude I was indistinguishable from a pile of rocks. For the next hour he circled the icecap, scanning its barren contours without success. But the pilot, to his credit, appreciated the gravity of my predicament and didn't give up. Frantic, I tied my sleeping bag to the end of one of the crevasse poles and waved it for all I was worth. When the plane banked sharply and began to fly straight at me, I felt tears of joy well in my eyes.

The pilot buzzed my tent three times in quick succession, dropping two boxes on each pass, then the airplane disappeared over a ridge and I was alone. As silence again settled over the glacier I felt abandoned, vulnerable, lost. I realized that I was sobbing. Embarrassed, I halted the blubbering by screaming obscenities until I grew hoarse.

I awoke early on May 11 to clear skies and the relatively warm temperature of twenty degrees Fahrenheit. Startled by the good weather, mentally unprepared to commence the actual climb, I hurriedly packed up a rucksack nonetheless, and began skiing toward the base of the Thumb. Two previous Alaskan expeditions had taught me that, ready or not, you simply can't afford to waste a day of perfect weather if you expect to get up anything.

A small hanging glacier extends out from the lip of the icecap, leading up and across the north face of the Thumb like a catwalk. My plan was to follow this catwalk to a prominent rock prow in the center of the wall, and thereby execute an end run around the ugly, avalanche-swept lower half of the face.

The catwalk turned out to be a series of fifty-degree ice fields blanketed with knee-deep powder snow and riddled with crevasses. The depth of the snow made the going slow and exhausting; by the time I front-pointed up the overhanging wall of the uppermost *bergschrund*, some three or four hours after leaving camp, I was whipped. And I hadn't even gotten to the "real" climbing yet. That would begin immediately above, where the hanging glacier gave way to vertical rock.

The rock, exhibiting a dearth of holds and coated with six inches of crumbly rime, did not look promising, but just left of the main prow was an inside corner—what climbers call an open book—

glazed with frozen melt water. This ribbon of ice led straight up for two or three hundred feet, and if the ice proved substantial enough to support the picks of my ice axes, the line might go. I hacked out a small platform in the snow slope, the last flat ground I expected to feel underfoot for some time, and stopped to eat a candy bar and collect my thoughts. Fifteen minutes later I shouldered my pack and inched over to the bottom of the corner. Gingerly, I swung my right axe into the two-inch-thick ice. It was solid, plastic—a little thinner than I would have liked but otherwise perfect. I was on my way.

The climbing was steep and spectacular, so exposed it made my head spin. Beneath my boot soles, the wall fell away for three thousand feet to the dirty, avalanche-scarred cirque of the Witches Cauldron Glacier. Above, the prow soared with authority toward the summit ridge, a vertical half-mile above. Each time I planted one of my ice axes, that distance shrank by another twenty inches.

The higher I climbed, the more comfortable I became. All that held me to the mountainside, all that held me to the world, were six thin spikes of chrome-molybdenum stuck half an inch into a smear of frozen water, yet I began to feel invincible, weightless, like those lizards that live on the ceilings of cheap Mexican hotels. Early on a difficult climb, especially a difficult solo climb, you're hyperaware of the abyss pulling at your back. You constantly feel its call, its immense hunger. To resist takes a tremendous conscious effort; you don't dare let your guard down for an instant. The siren song of the void puts you on edge, it makes your movements tentative, clumsy, herky-jerky. But as the climb goes on, you grow accustomed to the exposure, you get used to rubbing shoulders with doom, you come to believe in the reliability of your hands and feet and head. You learn to trust your self-control.

By and by, your attention becomes so intensely focused that you no longer notice the raw knuckles, the cramping thighs, the strain of maintaining nonstop concentration. A trance-like state settles over your efforts, the climb becomes a clear-eyed dream. Hours

△ 175

slide by like minutes. The accrued guilt and clutter of day-to-day existence—the lapses of conscience, the unpaid bills, the bungled opportunities, the dust under the couch, the festering familial sores, the inescapable prison of your genes—all of it is temporarily forgotten, crowded from your thoughts by an overpowering clarity of purpose, and by the seriousness of the task at hand.

At such moments, something like happiness actually stirs in your chest, but it isn't the sort of emotion you want to lean on very hard. In solo climbing, the whole enterprise is held together with little more than chutzpa, not the most reliable adhesive. Late in the day on the north face of the Thumb, I felt the glue disintegrate with a single swing of an ice axe.

I'd gained nearly seven hundred feet of altitude since stepping off the hanging glacier, all of it on crampon front-points and the picks of my axes. The ribbon of frozen melt water had ended three hundred feet up, and was followed by a crumbly armor of frost feathers. Though just barely substantial enough to support body weight, the rime was plastered over the rock to a thickness of two or three feet, so I kept plugging upward. The wall, however, had been growing imperceptibly steeper, and as it did so the frost feathers became thinner. I'd fallen into a slow, hypnotic rhythm—swing, swing; kick, kick; swing, swing; kick, kick—when my left ice axe slammed into a slab of diorite a few inches beneath the rime.

I tried left, then right, but kept striking rock. The frost feathers holding me up, it became apparent, were maybe five inches thick and had the structural integrity of stale cornbread. Below was thirty-seven hundred feet of air, and I was balanced atop a house of cards. Waves of panic rose in my throat. My eyesight blurred, I began to hyperventilate, my calves started to vibrate. I shuffled a few feet farther to the right, hoping to find thicker ice, but managed only to bend an ice axe on the rock.

Awkwardly, stiff with fear, I started working my way back down. The rime gradually thickened, and after descending about eighty feet I got back on reasonably solid ground. I stopped for a long time to let my nerves settle, then leaned back from my tools and stared up at the face above, searching for a hint of solid ice, for some variation in the underlying rock strata, for anything that would allow passage over the frosted slabs. I looked until my neck ached, but nothing appeared. The climb was over. The only place to go was down.

Heavy snow and incessant winds kept me inside the tent for most of the next three days. The hours passed slowly. In the attempt to hurry them along I chain-smoked for as long as my supply of cigarettes held out, and read. I'd made a number of bad decisions on the trip, there was no getting around it, and one of them concerned the reading matter I'd chosen to pack along: three back issues of _The Village Voice_, and Joan Didion's latest novel, _A Book of Common Prayer_. The _Voice_ was amusing enough—there on the icecap, the subject matter took on an edge, a certain sense of the absurd, from which the paper (through no fault of its own) benefited greatly— but in that tent, under those circumstances, Didion's necrotic take on the world hit a little too close to home.

Near the end of _Common Prayer_, one of Didion's characters says to another, "You don't get any real points for staying here, Charlotte." Charlotte replies, "I can't seem to tell what you do get real points for, so I guess I'll stick around here for awhile."

When I ran out of things to read, I was reduced to studying the ripstop pattern woven into the tent ceiling. This I did for hours on end, flat on my back, while engaging in an extended and very heated self-debate: Should I leave for the coast as soon as the weather broke, or stay put long enough to make another attempt on the mountain? In truth, my little escapade on the north face had left me badly shaken, and I didn't want to go up on the Thumb again at all. On the other hand, the thought of returning to Boulder in defeat—of parking the Pontiac behind the trailer, buckling on my tool belt, and going back to the same brain-dead drill I'd so triumphantly walked away from just a month before—that wasn't very

△ 177

appealing, either. Most of all, I couldn't stomach the thought of having to endure the smug expressions of condolence from all the chumps and nimrods who were certain I'd fail right from the get-go.

By the third afternoon of the storm I couldn't stand it any longer: the lumps of frozen snow poking me in the back, the clammy nylon walls brushing against my face, the incredible smell drifting up from the depths of my sleeping bag. I pawed through the mess at my feet until I located a small green stuff sack, in which there was a metal film can containing the makings of what I'd hoped would be a sort of victory cigar. I'd intended to save it for my return from the summit, but what the hey, it wasn't looking like I'd be visiting the top any time soon. I poured most of the can's contents onto a leaf of cigarette paper, rolled it into a crooked, sorry looking joint, and promptly smoked it down to the roach.

The reefer, of course, only made the tent seem even more cramped, more suffocating, more impossible to bear. It also made me terribly hungry. I decided a little oatmeal would put things right. Making it, however, was a long, ridiculously involved process: a potful of snow had to be gathered outside in the tempest, the stove assembled and lit, the oatmeal and sugar located, the remnants of yesterday's dinner scraped from my bowl. I'd gotten the stove going and was melting the snow when I smelled something burning. A thorough check of the stove and its environs revealed nothing. Mystified, I was ready to chalk it up to my chemically enhanced imagination when I heard something crackle directly behind me.

I whirled around in time to see a bag of garbage, into which I'd tossed the match I'd used to light the stove, flare up into a conflagration. Beating on the fire with my hands, I had it out in a few seconds, but not before a large section of the tent's inner wall vaporized before my eyes. The tent's built-in rainfly escaped the flames, so the shelter was still more or less weatherproof; now, however, it was approximately thirty degrees cooler inside. My left palm began to sting. Examining it, I noticed the pink welt of a burn. What troubled me most, though, was that the tent wasn't even mine—I'd borrowed the shelter from my father. An expensive Early Winters OmnipoTent, it had been brand new before my trip—the hang-tags were still attached—and had been loaned reluctantly. For several minutes I sat dumbstruck, staring at the wreckage of the shelter's once-graceful form amid the acrid scent of singed hair and melted nylon. You had to hand it to me, I thought: I had a real knack for living up to the old man's worst expectations.

The fire sent me into a funk that no drug known to man could have alleviated. By the time I'd finished cooking the oatmeal my mind was made up: the moment the storm was over, I was breaking camp and booking for Thomas Bay.

Twenty-four hours later, I was huddled inside a bivouac sack under the lip of the *bergschrund* on the Thumb's north face. The weather was as bad as I'd seen it. It was snowing hard, probably an inch every hour. Spindrift avalanches hissed down from the wall above and washed over me like surf, completely burying the sack every twenty minutes.

The day had begun well enough. When I emerged from the tent, clouds still clung to the ridge tops but the wind was down and the icecap was speckled with sunbreaks. A patch of sunlight, almost blinding in its brilliance, slid lazily over the camp. I put down a foam sleeping mat and sprawled on the glacier in my long johns. Wallowing in the radiant heat, I felt the gratitude of a prisoner whose sentence has just been commuted.

As I lay there, a narrow chimney that curved up the east half of the Thumb's north face, well to the left of the route I'd tried before the storm, caught my eye. I twisted a telephoto lens onto my camera. Through it I could make out a smear of shiny grey ice—solid, trustworthy, hard-frozen ice—plastered to the back of the cleft. The alignment of the chimney made it impossible to discern if the ice continued in an unbroken line from top to bottom. If it

△ 179

did, the chimney might well provide passage over the rime-covered slabs that had foiled my first attempt. Lying there in the sun, I began to think about how much I'd hate myself a month hence if I threw in the towel after a single try, if I scrapped the whole expedition on account of a little bad weather. Within the hour I had assembled my gear and was skiing toward the base of the wall.

The ice in the chimney did in fact prove to be continuous, but it was very, very thin—just a gossamer film of verglas. Additionally, the cleft was a natural funnel for any debris that happened to slough off the wall; as I scratched my way up the chimney I was hosed by a continuous stream of powder snow, ice chips, and small stones. One hundred twenty feet up the groove the last remnants of my composure flaked away like old plaster, and I turned around.

Instead of descending all the way to base camp, I decided to spend the night in the 'schrund beneath the chimney, on the off chance that my head would be more together the next morning. The fair skies that had ushered in the day, however, turned out to be but a momentary lull in a five-day gale. By midafternoon the storm was back in all its glory, and my bivouac site became a less than pleasant place to hang around. The ledge on which I crouched was continually swept by small spindrift avalanches. Five times my bivvy sack—a thin nylon envelope, shaped exactly like a Baggies brand sandwich bag, only bigger—was buried up to the level of the breathing slit. After digging myself out the fifth time, I decided I'd had enough. I threw all my gear in my pack and made a break for base camp.

The descent was terrifying. Between the clouds, the ground blizzard, and the flat, fading light, I couldn't tell snow from sky, nor whether a slope went up or down. I worried, with ample reason, that I might step blindly off the top of a serac and end up at the bottom of the Witches Cauldron, a half-mile below. When I finally arrived on the frozen plain of the icecap, I found that my tracks had long since drifted over. I didn't have a clue how to locate the tent on the featureless glacial plateau. I skied in circles for an hour or so, hoping I'd get lucky and stumble across camp, until I put a foot into a small crevasse and realized I was acting like an idiot—that I should hunker down right where I was and wait out the storm.

I dug a shallow hole, wrapped myself in the bivvy bag, and sat on my pack in the swirling snow. Drifts piled up around me. My feet became numb. A damp chill crept down my chest from the base of my neck, where spindrift had gotten inside my parka and soaked my shirt. If only I had a cigarette, I thought, a single cigarette, I could summon the strength of character to put a good face on this fucked-up situation, on the whole fucked-up trip. "If we had some ham, we could have ham and eggs, if we had some eggs." I remembered my friend Nate uttering that line in a similar storm, two years before, high on another Alaskan peak, the Mooses Tooth. It had struck me as hilarious at the time; I'd actually laughed out loud. Recalling the line now, it no longer seemed funny. I pulled the bivvy sack tighter around my shoulders. The wind ripped at my back. Beyond shame, I cradled my head in my arms and embarked on an orgy of self-pity.

I knew that people sometimes died climbing mountains. But at the age of twenty-three personal mortality—the idea of my own death—was still largely outside my conceptual grasp; it was as abstract a notion as non-Euclidian geometry or marriage. When I decamped from Boulder in April, 1977, my head swimming with visions of glory and redemption on the Devils Thumb, it didn't occur to me that I might be bound by the same cause-effect relationships that governed the actions of others. I'd never heard of hubris. Because I wanted to climb the mountain so badly, because I had thought about the Thumb so intensely for so long, it seemed beyond the realm of possibility that some minor obstacle like the weather or crevasses or rime-covered rock might ultimately thwart my will.

At sunset the wind died and the ceiling lifted 150 feet off the glacier, enabling me to locate base camp. I made it back to the tent intact, but it was no longer possible to ignore the fact that the Thumb had made hash of my plans. I was forced to acknowledge that volition alone, however powerful, was not going to get me up the north wall. I saw, finally, that nothing was.

There still existed an opportunity for salvaging the expedition, however. A week earlier I'd skied over to the southeast side of the mountain to take a look at the route Fred Beckey had pioneered in 1946—the route by which I'd intended to descend the peak after climbing the north wall. During that reconnaissance I'd noticed an obvious unclimbed line to the left of the Beckey route—a patchy network of ice angling across the southeast face—that struck me as a relatively easy way to achieve the summit. At the time, I'd considered this route unworthy of my attentions. Now, on the rebound from my calamitous entanglement with the nordwand, I was prepared to lower my sights.

On the afternoon of May 15, when the blizzard finally petered out, I returned to the southeast face and climbed to the top of a slender ridge that abutted the upper peak like a flying buttress on a gothic cathedral. I decided to spend the night there, on the airy, knife-edged ridge crest, sixteen hundred feet below the summit. The evening sky was cold and cloudless. I could see all the way to tidewater and beyond. At dusk I watched, transfixed, as the house lights of Petersburg blinked on in the west. The closest thing I'd had to human contact since the airdrop, the distant lights set off a flood of emotion that caught me completely off guard. I imagined people watching the Red Sox on the tube, eating fried chicken in brightly lit kitchens, drinking beer, making love. When I lay down to sleep I was overcome by a soul-wrenching loneliness. I'd never felt so alone, ever.

That night I had troubled dreams, of cops and vampires and a gangland-style execution. I heard someone whisper, "He's in there. As soon as he comes out, waste him." I sat bolt upright and opened my eyes. The sun was about to rise. The entire sky was scarlet.

△ 182

It was still clear, but wisps of high cirrus were streaming in from the southwest, and a dark line was visible just above the horizon. I pulled on my boots and hurriedly strapped on my crampons. Five minutes after waking up, I was front-pointing away from the bivouac.

I carried no rope, no tent or bivouac gear, no hardware save my ice axes. My plan was to go ultralight and ultrafast, to hit the summit and make it back down before the weather turned. Pushing myself, continually out of breath, I hurried up and to the left across small snowfields linked by narrow runnels of verglas and short rock bands. The climbing was almost fun—the rock was covered with large, in-cut holds, and the ice, though thin, never got steep enough to feel extreme—but I was anxious about the bands of clouds racing in from the Pacific, covering the sky.

In what seemed like no time (I didn't have a watch on the trip) I was on the distinctive final ice field. By now the sky was completely overcast. It looked easier to keep angling to the left, but quicker to go straight for the top. Paranoid about being caught by a storm high on the peak without any kind of shelter, I opted for the direct route. The ice steepened, then steepened some more, and as it did so it grew thin. I swung my left ice axe and struck rock. I aimed for another spot, and once again it glanced off unyielding diorite with a dull, sickening clank. And again, and again: It was a reprise of my first attempt on the north face. Looking between my legs, I stole a glance at the glacier, more than two thousand feet below. My stomach churned. I felt my poise slipping away like smoke in the wind.

Forty-five feet above the wall eased back onto the sloping summit shoulder. Forty-five more feet, half the distance between third base and home plate, and the mountain would be mine. I clung stiffly to my axes, unmoving, paralyzed with fear and indecision. I looked down at the dizzying drop to the glacier again, then up, then scraped away the film of ice above my head. I hooked the pick of my left axe on a nickel-thin lip of rock, and weighted it. It held. I pulled

△ 183

my right axe from the ice, reached up, and twisted the pick into a crooked half-inch crack until it jammed. Barely breathing now, I moved my feet up, scrabbling my crampon points across the verglas. Reaching as high as I could with my left arm, I swung the axe gently at the shiny, opaque surface, not knowing what I'd hit beneath it. The pick went in with a heartening *THUNK*! A few minutes later I was standing on a broad, rounded ledge. The summit proper, a series of slender fins sprouting a grotesque meringue of atmospheric ice, stood twenty feet directly above.

The insubstantial frost feathers ensured that those last twenty feet remained hard, scary, onerous. But then, suddenly, there was no place higher to go. It wasn't possible, I couldn't believe it. I felt my cracked lips stretch into a huge, painful grin. I was on top of the Devils Thumb.

Fittingly, the summit was a surreal, malevolent place, an improbably slender fan of rock and rime no wider than a filing cabinet. It did not encourage loitering. As I straddled the highest point, the north face fell away beneath my left boot for six thousand feet; beneath my right boot the south face dropped off for twenty-five hundred. I took some pictures to prove I'd been there, and spent a few minutes trying to straighten a bent pick. Then I stood up, carefully turned around, and headed for home.

Five days later I was camped in the rain beside the sea, marveling at the sight of moss, willows, mosquitoes. Two days after that, a small skiff motored into Thomas Bay and pulled up on the beach not far from my tent. The man driving the boat introduced himself as Jim Freeman, a timber faller from Petersburg. It was his day off, he said, and he'd made the trip to show his family the glacier, and to look for bears. He asked me if I'd "been huntin', or what?"

"No," I replied sheepishly. "Actually, I just climbed the Devils Thumb. I've been over here twenty days."

Freeman kept fiddling with a cleat on the boat, and didn't say anything for a while. Then he looked at me real hard and spat,

"You wouldn't be givin' me double talk now, wouldja, friend?" Taken aback, I stammered out a denial. Freeman, it was obvious, didn't believe me for a minute. Nor did he seem wild about my snarled shoulder-length hair or the way I smelled. When I asked if he could give me a lift back to town, however, he offered a grudging, "I don't see why not."

The water was choppy, and the ride across Frederick Sound took two hours. The more we talked, the more Freeman warmed up. He still didn't believe I'd climbed the Thumb, but by the time he steered the skiff into Wrangell Narrows he pretended to. When we got off the boat, he insisted on buying me a cheeseburger. That night he even let me sleep in a derelict step-van parked in his backyard.

I lay down in the rear of the old truck for a while but couldn't sleep, so I got up and walked to a bar called Kito's Kave. The euphoria, the overwhelming sense of relief, that had initially accompanied my return to Petersburg faded, and an unexpected melancholy took its place. The people I chatted with in Kito's didn't seem to doubt that I'd been to the top of the Thumb, they just didn't much care. As the night wore on the place emptied except for me and an Indian at a back table. I drank alone, putting quarters in the jukebox, playing the same five songs over and over, until the barmaid yelled angrily, "Hey! Give it a fucking rest, kid! If I hear 'Fifty Ways to Lose Your Lover' one more time, *I'm* gonna be the one who loses it." I mumbled an apology, quickly headed for the door, and lurched back to Freeman's step-van. There, surrounded by the sweet scent of old motor oil, I lay down on the floorboards next to a gutted transmission and passed out.

It is easy, when you are young, to believe that what you desire is no less than what you deserve, to assume that if you want something badly enough it is your God-given right to have it. Less than a month after sitting on the summit of the Thumb I was back in Boulder, nailing up siding on the Spruce Street Townhouses, the same condos I'd been framing when I left for Alaska. I got a raise,

△ 185

to four dollars an hour, and at the end of the summer moved out of the job-site trailer to a studio apartment on West Pearl, but little else in my life seemed to change. Somehow, it didn't add up to the glorious transformation I'd imagined in April.

Climbing the Devils Thumb, however, had nudged me a little further away from the obdurate innocence of childhood. It taught me something about what mountains can and can't do, about the limits of dreams. I didn't recognize that at the time, of course, but I'm grateful for it now.